Walk in My Presence

Nicholas Hutchinson FSC

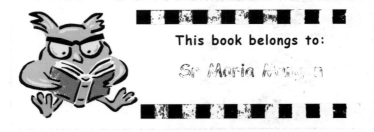

This book belongs to:

Sr Maria Ming, o

Matthew James Publishing Ltd

Also available by the same author:

Praying Each Day of the Year (1997-1998)

– a 3 volume series that offers a reflection and prayer specific to the anniversaries of events.

1 898366 30 6 – Volume 1: (January to April)
1 898366 31 4 – Volume 2: (May to August)
1 898366 32 2 – Volume 3: (September to December)

Lord, Teach us to Pray (1999)

- a 50 day course of personal prayer, exploring various ways of praying through creative use of Scripture and imagery.
1 898366 65 9 Lord, Teach us to Pray

Published by
Matthew James Publishing Ltd,
19 Wellington Close,
Chelmsford, Essex CM1 2EE

ISBN 1 898366 60 8

First published 2002

Cover design by Peter Robb
Typeset by Linda East
Printed by J W Arrowsmith, Bristol

Dedicated to the memory of
Brother Edwin Bannon, FSC
(1917-2001)
who inspired and encouraged many
to touch the hearts and minds
of people of all ages

Contents

Foreword

The vivid and evocative imagery of *'walking with God'* is first encountered in the Book of Genesis. There we read that figures such as Abraham and Joseph *'walked with God'*[1], and God makes a promise to Eli: *"Your House… will walk in my presence for ever."*[2]

In a poetic way the psalms describe our relationship as *'walking in the presence of God'*[3]. and we pray: *'Lord, teach me how to walk beside you faithfully'*[4]. These words are particularly poignant as a new day begins, and we ask that our eyes be opened to recognise the Risen Jesus, as happened to the two frightened disciples whose world had collapsed around them[5]. Jesus joined them and walked by their side but, at first, something prevented them from recognising him. As their eyes were opened, much fell into place and they knew that all manner of thing would be well. Their hearts were on fire as Jesus engaged them in conversation on the road and explained the scriptures to them.

For many Christians this remains one of the most prayed-over passages in the Gospels. The disciples' two-hour walk of discovery from Jerusalem to the village of Emmaus became the summit of their lifetime of exploring. It was as though they had arrived where they had started and knew the place for the first time[6]. That journey mirrors our searching each day with our own *'joys and hopes, and grief and anxiety… in our pilgrimage towards the Father's kingdom'*[7].

In that spirit, may all of us who use this book pray for one another and grow in compassion as companions who are sharing the same journey – that of 'the pilgrim people of God'[8] – knowing that, if we have eyes to see, we can discover that *'Earth's crammed with heaven and every bush is afire with God'*[9].

> **Brother Jesus,**
> **your presence is interwoven**
> **throughout each day of our lives.**
> **As we journey with our fellow pilgrims,**
> **touch our hearts and open our eyes**
> **that we may recognise you**
> **walking beside us.**
> **Lead us to live in such a way**
> **that we discover you**
> **in the quietness and in the spaces,**
> **as well as in the busyness**
> **of our lives each day.**
> **Continue to call us your friends**
> **and accompany us**
> **to where we shall see our Father, face to face.**
> **Amen.**

---

1 – Gen 5[22], 6[9], 24[40], 48[15]; **2** – 1 Sam 2[30]; **3** – Ps 119[9]; **4** – Ps 56[13], 86[11]; **5** – Lk 24[13-35];
6 – cf. T.S. Eliot: *Little Gidding* V; **7** – Vatican II: Gaudium et Spes, 1; **8** – Vatican II: Lumen Gentium, 68;
9 – Elizabeth Barrett Browning: Aurora Leigh, bk. 7, l. 821

WALK IN MY PRESENCE

Introduction

Many people put to good use collections of prayers as well as anthologies of readings, but there are very few books – like this – of prayer services of themed prayers and readings. Draft copies of these prayer services have been very well-received, and I have been grateful for the constructive comments that people have offered. Amongst those who are likely to find this book of help will be parish and retreat groups of all ages, catechists, teachers with older students, religious communities, and individuals in various circumstances. Those looking for prayer services for the Church's Year will find them in the second volume of *Walk In My Presence* which will be available for Advent 2002.

Gathering in the Presence of God

The focus of these prayer services is such that each begins very clearly with the life-giving practice of reminding ourselves that we are in the Presence of God. We appreciate that it is not that we are *placing* ourselves in God's Presence; rather we are focussing on where we are already. God makes his home with us, abides with us, is to be found in our midst, is present when two or three gather in His name[1]. He promises to be with us always, for it is in him that we live and move and have our being[2].

Celtic and many other spiritualities focus on God's Presence, God-being-with-us in the ordinariness of daily life. The beautiful craftsmanship of Celtic manuscripts and crosses showing intertwining paths, draws us to focus on God's Presence being 'woven' throughout all the strands of our lives. Ongoing renewal of a sense of the Presence of God is essential for our walking with God: that warm relationship in which we are called *'friends of God'*[3] and *'see him face-to-face'*[4].

With the emphasis on initially reminding ourselves that God is with us, it is best that a hymn not precede the *Gathering in the Presence of God*, but be sung later at an appropriate time. At the back of the book (pg 121ff) some suitable hymns are listed for each prayer service, and I am reminded that one of the notes written by Johann Sebastian Bach (1685-1750) in the margins of his Bible, reads: *"Where there is devotional music, God with his grace is always present!"* And some will recall that Augustine commented that *"the one who sings well, prays twice!"*

The Need for Pauses

Words of the fourth verse (usually omitted from hymn books) of John Whittier's *Dear Lord and Father of mankind* remind us that other things – though often important – can obscure our need to pause and meet God in prayer:

> *"…All our words and works that drown*
> *The tender whisper of Thy call…"*

A choice has been made that each of the thirty prayer services that form this book not be of too many words, lest the length promote a feeling of a need to 'get through' what is printed. Any such sense of haste would detract from one of the essential 'ingredients' of a prayer service, namely of having pauses, spaces: the better to slow down, reflect, sensitise ourselves and encourage us to 'allow' God opportunities to 'slip in'. "*The Divine Presence slips through the crevices between our words and judgements. Wall-to-wall spiritual talk leaves no oxygen for a living God to breathe*" (pg 274 of Eternal Echoes by John O'Donohue, Bantam Books).

Having avoided overcrowding of material also helps to convey that praying is not necessarily the same as saying prayers! We use words when helpful, but appreciate the need to allow God also to work through silence. All who are in love appreciate that much time is of silent pauses – not of nothingness, but of quiet time that reflects the warmth of a loving relationship in which words, though important, are not always necessary. Pausing also alerts us to have the attitude of listening, of being aware, of being open.

Selecting Materials

There is no need, of course, to use everything that is printed in a particular prayer service. The aim is to pray, and not necessarily to use all the words that are provided!

For convenience, sections of longer prayers have been numbered so as to be of help if taken in turn by two groups. Numbering may also assist the sharing of lengthier readings. If readers know passages in advance, it is an encouragement for them to ponder and pray the reading before presenting it to the group. The numbering of items in the main text is discreet, reminding us that the book is designed to be very much more than an anthology of inspiring pieces: these are prayer services. Likewise, although authors are named beside texts, the precise source is listed at the back of the book (pg 129ff) so as to minimise distractions during the time of prayer.

Not all of the services include prayers of intercession. If it is decided to include a period of time for such spontaneous prayers, it is advisable before starting the prayer service to announce at what point that will be. Some people choose the Lord's Prayer to conclude a time of intercession.

Each service concludes specifically with a blessing, which may also serve to give a clear indication that the prayer service has come to an end. Most of these blessings are based on Scripture, from which much inspiration for the contents of this book has been derived.

One appendix offers a means to locate passages throughout each book of the Bible. Many people have commented how useful they have found this to be, and it is re-printed from *Praying Each Day of the Year*, by the same author and publisher. The index is fulsome as a help to locating passages that become familiar.

A Way of Praying – especially with Scripture

Confronted these days with 'information overload', many of us feel the need for scanning and speed reading as a means of detecting points in a text, or of judging which paragraphs should be read in full. There is a danger if we transfer this approach to the reading of the Scriptures. Far from seeking to glean *information*, we are aiming for *formation* of God's Word deep within. For too long there was a tendency to perceive the Scriptures simply as containing a moral or doctrinal message. Once such a 'message' had been 'picked up', some thought that the 'static' text had achieved its purpose. Yet '*the word of God is alive and active*'[5], as many come to know in their own lives.

As I pray in the simplicity of our own chapel, I find it very helpful that two spotlights have a particular focus: one on the Body of the Lord, reserved in one corner at the front, and another on the enthroned, open Word of the Lord in the other. Indeed, *'the Church has always venerated the Divine Scriptures just as it has venerated the Body of the Lord'*[6].

The process of repeating a passage slowly (preferably whispering it aloud, if alone, helping to sense both listening and proclamation), pondering it, and dwelling particularly on a couple of phrases, encourages us to allow the words to enter deep within us. There - and this is especially the case with Scripture – the Spirit can give flesh to that word and transform us to become more like the Father. This way of praying (a form of *Lectio Divina*, which can be explored readily on the Internet) is a means of 'allowing' God to touch our hearts and embrace us.

The key verb *to listen* (implying a knowing and realising deep within), occurs some 445 times through the Bible (JB). Conscious of the Lord's call for *"those who have ears to hear, to listen"*[7], we pray to be open to hear *'the still, small voice of God'*[8]. Our prayer is *"Speak, Lord, you servant is listening"*[9]. Having listened and heard and then *'pondered the words in our hearts'*[10], we pray for its fulfilment in our daily lives. *'As the rain and the snow come down from the heavens and do not return without watering the earth, so may God's word not return to him empty without carrying out his will, but succeed in what it was sent to do.'*[11] Lord, *"be it done to me according to your word."*[12]

A Conclusion

The world's largest Gothic arches in Liverpool's Anglican Cathedral help convey for me something of the magnificence of God. Yet their architect, Sir Giles Gilbert Scott, remarked: *"Do not look at my arches, but at the spaces they create."* It is hoped that this book may help us to dwell amongst the 'spaces' created, as well as in the words we use: giving an opportunity for the God of spaces to dwell fully in us and amongst us, filling whatever emptiness he finds there. May we be *'filled with the utter fullness of God'*.[13]

Brother Nicholas Hutchinson FSC
De La Salle House
83 Carr Lane East
Liverpool
L11 4SF
email: nicholas@prayingeachday.org
website: www.prayingeachday.org

---

1 – Jn 14[23], 15[3], 19[8], Mt 18[20]; **2** – Mt 28[20], Acts 17[28]; **3** – Wis 7[27], Jam 2[23];
4 – Gen 32[31], Ex 33[11], Num 14[14], Is 52[8], Rev 22[4]; **5** – Heb 4[12]; **6** – Vatican II: Dei Verbum, 21; **7** – Mt
11[15]; **8** – 1 Kings 19[12]; **9** – 1 Sam 3[10]; **10** – cf. Lk 2[19];
11 – cf. Is 55[10-11]; **12** – Lk 1[38]; **13** – Eph 3[19]

Gathering in the Presence of God
David Adam   **1**

The history of salvation and incarnation has to become our own personal history.
The Celtic way of always inviting God into their activities, and seeking to become
aware of him in everyday events, is the most natural way of achieving this. Here
we have a weaving of God's Presence around our lives like the Celtic patterns on
stones and in the illuminated Gospels: Christ moves in and out, over and under.
We are encircled by him, encompassed by his presence and love.

Let us remind ourselves
that we are already in the presence of God
ALL   and let us adore him.

(pause)

Prayer
attributed to St Patrick   **2**

Christ be with me, Christ within me,
Christ behind me, Christ before me,
Christ beside me, Christ to win me,
Christ to comfort and restore me.
Christ beneath me, Christ above me,
Christ in quiet, Christ in danger,
Christ in hearts of all that love me,
Christ in mouth of friend and stranger.

(pause)

Reading
Thomas Merton   **3**

Sunrise is an event that calls forth solemn music in the very depth of human
nature, as if one's whole being had to attune itself to the cosmos and praise God
for the new day: praising God in the name of all the creatures that ever were, or
ever will be. I look at the rising sun, and feel that now upon me falls the
responsibility of seeing what all my ancestors have seen, in the Stone Age and
even before it, praising God before me… When the sun rises, each one of us is
summoned by the living and the dead to praise God.

4 Prayer
from the Armenian
Liturgy

    Lord God, Creator of light,
    at the rising of your sun each morning
    let the greatest of all lights – your love –
    rise like the sun within my heart.

5 Psalm 113

Antiphon: The lands of sunrise and sunset you fill with your joy.

    Praise, O servants of the Lord,
    praise the name of the Lord!
    May the name of the Lord be blessed
    both now and for evermore!
    From the rising of the sun to its setting
    praised be the name of the Lord!

    High above all nations is the Lord,
    above the heavens his glory.
    Who is like the Lord, our God,
    who has risen on high to his throne
    yet stoops from the heights to look down,
    to look down upon heaven and earth?

    From the dust he lifts up the lowly,
    from the dungheap he raises the poor
    to set them in the company of rulers,
    yes, with the rulers of his people.
    To the childless wife he gives a home
    and gladdens her heart with children.

    Glory be…

Antiphon: The lands of sunrise and sunset you fill with your joy.
        (Ps 65⁸)

6 Reading
    John Powell, SJ

It is obvious to me that each new day – along with all the persons and events of
that day – does in fact question us, if we will submit to the test. The needy,
unattractive person asks me how much I can love. The death of a dear one asks
me what I really believe about death, and how profitably I can confront loss and
loneliness. A beautiful day and a beautiful person ask me how capable I am of
enjoyment. Solitude asks me if I really like myself and enjoy my own company.
A good joke asks me if I have a sense of humour. A very different type of person
from a background very dissimilar to my own, asks me if I am capable of empathy

    WALK IN MY PRESENCE

and understanding. Success and failure ask me to define my ideas of success and failure. Suffering asks me if I really believe I can grow through adversity. Negative criticism directed to me, asks me about my sensitivities and self-confidence. The devotion and commitment of another to me, asks me if I will let myself be loved.

Prayer NH 7

Lord Jesus,
    I ask for the power of your Spirit
    that I may remain positive
    throughout all that happens
    each day of my life,
    knowing that nothing
    can ever separate me
    from your love.
I know that your touch
    can change people and situations,
    and so I ask you
    to join me in offering to our Father
    not only the good things of this day,
    but also any suffering and sacrifices
    that I want to offer
    cheerfully and lovingly,
    and in a quiet and hidden way.
And so may any difficulties
    and frustration and pain of this day
    be transformed in your presence
    for the benefit of other people. Amen.

Blessing A Celtic Blessing 8

1 May God's Spirit guide us
    and lead us to see in what we do
    the beauty of our own souls.

2 May the work that we do
    with the secret love and warmth of our heart
    be blessed by him.
    May it be God's work.

3 May the sacredness of God's work
    bring healing, light and renewal
    to those who work with us
    and to those who see and receive our work.
    May that work never weary us

but release within us
wellsprings of refreshment, inspiration and excitement.

4   May the morning find us awake and alert,
     approaching God's new day
     with dreams, possibilities and promises.

5   May evening find us gracious and fulfilled.
     May we go into the night
     blessed, sheltered and protected,
     and may God's Spirit calm, console and renew us. Amen.

The day ahead
– a morning prayer

Gathering in the Presence of God

9

Let us remind ourselves that God remembers us – he has written our names on the palm of his hands – and remains with us, as we pray together:

Sir Jacob Astley

Lord, help me today to realise
    that you will be speaking to me
    in various ways.
Give me ears, eyes and heart to perceive you,
    however veiled your presence may be.
Give me insight to see through what is exterior
    to what is within.
Give me your Spirit of discernment.

O Lord, you know how busy I must be this day.
If I forget you, do not forget me. Amen.

(pause)

Prayer

William Barclay   **10**

1   O God, I want to try to begin today
        by thinking not of myself but of others.
     Bless those for whom today is going to be a difficult day:
        those who must make decisions;
        those who must wrestle with temptations;
        those who have some special problem to solve.

2   Bless those for whom today is going to be a sad day:
        those who are meeting the day
           with tears in their eyes
           and with sorrow and loneliness in their hearts;
        those who today most lay some dear one to rest in death;
        those who awake to the morning with no work to do.

3   Bless those for whom today is going to be a happy day:
        those who are happy and who are eagerly looking forward to today;
        those who are to be married today;
        those who will walk in the sunshine of life today.

4   Give me all through today
      sympathy and love for all,
      that I may always try to weep with those who weep
      and rejoice with those who rejoice.
   Through Jesus Christ my Lord. Amen.

11   Reading

Teilhard de Chardin, SJ

God is not far away from us, is not apart from the world about us that we see, touch, hear, smell and taste. Rather, he awaits us at every instant in our action, in the work of the moment. There is a sense in which he is at the tip of my pen, my spade, my brush, my needle – of my heart and of my thought… By virtue of Creation – and still more of Incarnation – *nothing* here below is *profane* for those who know how to see. On the contrary, everything is sacred.

12   Prayer

'The Grail Prayer'

Lord Jesus,
I give you my hands, to do your work.
I give you my feet, to go your way.
I give you my eyes, to see as you do.
I give you my tongue, to speak your words.
I give you my mind, that you may think in me.
I give you my spirit, that you may pray in me.
Above all, I give you my heart
    that you may love, in me,
    your Father and all mankind.
I give you my whole self that you may grow in me
    so that it is you, Lord Jesus,
    who live and work and pray in me. Amen.

13   Personal Reflection

Rabindranath Tagore

Open your eyes and see…
God is there where the farmer is tilling the hard ground
and where the labourer is breaking stones.
He is with them in the sun and in the rain,
and his garment is covered with dust.
Put off your holy cloak
and, like him, come down onto the dusty soil.

14   Prayer

Misa Campesina

You are the God of the poor,
the simple and human God,
the God who sweats in the street,
the God with the weather-beaten face.

That's why I talk to you,
in the way that my people talk,
because you are the labourer God,
the worker Christ.

Prayer

C I Pettitt **15**

1   Lord, we bring our work to your working hands.
    We bring our sickness to your healing hands.

2   We bring our weakness to your strong hands.
    We bring our sadness to your tender hands.

3   We bring our needs to your praying hands.
    We bring our suffering to your wounded hands.

4   We bring our love, our families, and our children
    to your hands, outstretched to bless.

5   We bring our hands to share with you
    that Bread of Life which we take from you,
    that we may take your sacramental presence
    to share with others.

6   As we take your hands,
    we are to be those hands in the world today.

Reading

St Teresa of Avila **16**

Christ has no body now on earth but ours.
Ours are the only hands
    with which he can do his work.
Ours are the only feet
    with which he can go about doing good.
Ours are the only eyes
    through which his compassion
    can shine forth upon a troubled world.
Christ has no body now on earth but ours,
    and ours are the hands
    with which he is to bless others now.

Blessing

NH **17**

Remind us, Lord, that the end of our prayer
    is not the end of our time with you.
Our leaving you in prayer
    only brings us to join you once again
    in those to whom you send us.

Bless us at the start of this new day
    and bless the work and service of many kinds
    that we will do today.
Bless us, Father, Son and Holy Spirit,
    and continue – through us – to create, love and inspire,
    this day and always. Amen.

The journey to God
is a journey of discovery, full of surprises

Gathering in the Presence of God

Roger Schutz,
Prior of Taizé

18

Roger Schutz has written:

"Let yourself
be plumbed to the depths,
and you will realise
that everyone is created
for a presence.
There, in your heart of hearts,
in that place
where no two people are alike,
Christ is waiting for you.
And there
the unexpected happens."

Let us pause for each of us to recognise Christ in our heart of hearts.

(pause)

Prayer

based on a prayer of
St Augustine

19

You know, Lord, of my fruitless search
for what I had hoped might satisfy.
It is late that I have loved you,
O beauty ever-ancient, ever-new!
Behold, you were within, and I was without;
and it was without that I sought you.
And, deformed, I ran after
those forms of beauty you had made.
You were with me,
and I was not with you.

Help me to make the journey inward
and discover your kingdom within.
In the secret of my heart
I ask you to teach me wisdom. Amen.

20 Reading

Archbishop Anthony Bloom

The Gospel tells us that the Kingdom of God is within us first of all. If we cannot find the Kingdom of God within us, if we cannot meet God within, in the very depth of ourselves, our chances of meeting him outside ourselves are very remote. When Gagarin, the first astronaut, came back from space and made his remarkable statement that he never saw God in Heaven, one of our priests in Moscow remarked, *"If you have never seen him on earth, you will never see him in Heaven."* This is also true of what I am speaking about. If we cannot find a contact with God under our own skin, as it were, in this very small world in which I am, then the chances are very slight that, even if I meet him face to face, I will recognise him. St John Chrysostom said, *"Find the door of your heart; you will discover it is the door of the Kingdom of God."*

21 Reading and Prayer

Gerard Hughes, SJ

As I walked, the truth that God first loved us, and not for any merit of our own, broke in on me, and I wanted to laugh and cry at the same time at the wonder of it. I prayed:

> **ALL** Glory to you, O God, always greater.
> Touch me with your presence;
>   I want nothing else.
> Cleanse my mind and my heart
>   of false images of you
>   and put a new heart into me
>   which can know you in loving you.

22 Reading

Gerard Hughes, SJ

1 Our notion of God is mediated to us through parents, teachers and clergy… If our experience of parents and teachers has been of dominating people who show little affection or respect for us as persons, but value us only in so far as we conform to their expectations, then this experience is bound to affect our notion of God, and will influence the way we relate to him…

2 Although I may know in my mind that God is not like that, I may still experience a strong disinclination to approach him, without knowing why, and find a thousand reasons for not praying – I am too busy, I prefer to find him through my work, etc. We have to pray constantly to be rid of false notions of God, and we have to beg him to teach us who he is, for no one else can… What we are praying for is not merely an intellectual knowledge, but a felt knowledge which affects our whole being and therefore affects the way we see ourselves, other people, and the world around us.

To become aware that we have a distorted notion of God is to have made progress on our journey towards him… The journey to God is a journey of discovery, and it is full of surprises.

Prayer

You alone, Father,
> can change the false notions I have of you:
> many thoughts from my own experience
> of which I may now be unaware.

Reach deep within me and liberate me
> from whatever may distort
> your true likeness.

Bring me back – time and time again –
> to Jesus, your Son,
> in whose attitude and words and actions
> I can see clearly
> the perfect image of you, Father.

Reading

In prayer we undertake a vast journey from self to God. It is a journey that we cannot accomplish by our own efforts. We may start praying for very selfish motives, we may be looking for consolations, the satisfaction of being thought holy, an insurance policy for a happy hereafter – God in his mercy is very patient. He spoils us with consolations and joy. In time, though, he begins to prune, and prayer becomes dull and heavy. Alas, most give up at this moment. It really is a moment for growth. And so we need to know about the seasons of prayer, the good times and the difficult.

(pause)

Intercessions

1   Let us pray for the Lord's blessing on all who have helped us on our journey in life. Let us pray, too, that our hearts may be touched, so that we can be of help to others.
    Lord, in your mercy – ***hear our prayer***.

2   Let us pray that, in seeking the Lord, we may discover him as he really is, and realise that he is always present with us.
    Lord, in your mercy – ***hear our prayer***.

3   Let us pray for all who are searching and for all who are lost; for those who have given up hope, and for those who feel they have no-one to turn to.
    Lord, in your mercy – ***hear our prayer***.

4   Let us pray for people amidst anger and violence in their daily lives, that peace may be upon them.
    Lord, in your mercy – ***hear our prayer***.

26 **Blessing**

cf Colossians 1^{15,27}

May Christ,
the visible likeness of the invisible God,
keep our roots deep in him
and give us God's grace. Amen.

Gathering in the Presence of God

NH   27

It was through a garden courtyard that people entered some churches built at the time of the Roman Empire. The garden was to help people adjust from the busy day, and reflect on what they were about to do. It was an 'in-between place' of calm and peace, of beauty and quietness, enabling people to pause in time and space before entering the place of prayer. We, too, now pause to be calm and peaceful, and remind ourselves that God is with us.

(pause)

The Book of Genesis tells of God wanting to '*walk with Adam*' in the Garden of Eden, but Adam was hiding. God calls out to him: "*Where are you?*"

cf Gen 3[8-9]

In this introductory ('in-between') time, of starting our prayer, we focus on "*walking with God in the garden in the cool of the day*" and each of us, too, faces the question: "*Where am I in my life?*"

(pause)

Reading

Stephen Winward   28

Special times of prayer, whether in the quiet room or in the church, are not to be regarded as ends in themselves. They are not intended to be little islands of fellowship and peace, cut off from the great continent of ordinary life. This truth is finely expressed in the metaphor of '*walking with God*', which is found in many parts of the Bible. Two people walking together have the same destination, and the joy of companionship on the way towards it. They converse often together; and it is a two-way conversation of listening and speaking. At times they neither speak nor listen, but walk along together in silent thought, yet each fully aware of the presence of the other. So is communion with God. We have our regular times of private and public prayer, when we speak to him, and read and listen to his word. But these special times are only *part* of our communion. We are to be with him even when we are not speaking or listening to him.

Prayer

NH   29

Lord Jesus,
open our eyes to recognise you
as you walk beside us,
accompanying us
on our journey in life each day. Amen.

30 Personal Reflection

Stephen Winward

One thing we should do, is to take praying out into living. It is a mistake to confine prayer to the sacred times and places, the quiet room, the prayer group, the church. We must, of course, retire to pray, but it is no less important to pray in the actual setting of life's demands and events... Let us pray in life-situations, in the setting of events, so that praying and living may be one, woven together like the warp and weft of a garment.

31 Prayer

Karl Rahner, SJ

1 I now see clearly
   that, if there is any path at all
   on which I can approach you,
   it must lead through the very middle
   of my ordinary daily life.

2 If I should try to flee to you by any other way,
   I would actually be leaving myself behind,
   and that, aside from being quite impossible,
   would accomplish nothing at all...

3 Your love, which can allow my daily routine
   to remain routine and still transform it
   into a home-coming to you:
   this love only you can give.

4 As I come to lay my everyday routine before you,
   there is only one thing I beg for:
   and that is your most ordinary and most exalted gift:
   the grace of your love.

5 Touch my heart with this grace, O Lord.
   When I reach out in joy or in sorrow
   for the things of this world,
   grant that through them I may know and love you,
   their Maker and final home.

6 You who are Love itself,
   give me the grace of love, give me yourself,
   so that all my days may finally empty
   into the one day of your eternal Life.

Intercessions

1   We bring before you, Lord,
   all who will be making journeys today.
   We pray for young people on their way
   to school, college and university,
   and for those starting on a new stage of life's journey.
   Lord, in your mercy – ***hear our prayer***.

2   We pray, Lord,
   for those who are going to a new job,
   for those who seek work but have no job to journey to,
   and for those who are going to work for the last time.
   Lord, in your mercy – ***hear our prayer***.

3   We pray, Lord,
   for those starting a new life as they move house,
   for those who are afraid ever to leave their home,
   and for people who will be going into hospital today.
   Lord, in your mercy – ***hear our prayer***.

4   We pray, Lord,
   for those in the emergency services
   who will travel at speed on land, water or in the air
   and will place themselves in danger
   to bring help to others.
   Lord, in your mercy – ***hear our prayer***.

5   We pray, Lord,
   for prisoners who are travelling today,
   and for people who are homeless
   whose journey never takes them home.
   We pray for those who are lost on life's journey,
   and for those who cannot manage.
   Lord, in your mercy – ***hear our prayer***.

6   We pray, Lord,
   for those who will take further steps today
   on their journey of faith,
   and we pray for those who will die this day
   and make their final journey.
   On all these people
   we ask your blessing, Lord.
   Lord, in your mercy – ***hear our prayer***.

33 Blessing

Lord, make your home in us
and bring us once again the grace of your love.
Walk beside us this day
and bless us all the ways that we go:
in the name of the Father,
and of the Son
and of the Holy Spirit. Amen.

Gathering in the Presence of God

John Baptist De La Salle wrote that

*"reminding yourself of God's presence
will be a great advantage
in helping you and in inspiring you
to do everything well."*

And so let us remember that we are in the Presence of God
ALL   and let us adore him.

(pause)

Prayer

O God, it is easy to love the whole world,
   but hard to love the person one works next to.
O God, it is easy to campaign for world peace,
   but hard to contribute to the peace within my own home.
O God, it is easy to be fascinated with some new truth,
   and miss you in the thing I have known for so long.
O God, it is easy
   to share my home and possessions with people I like;
   teach me how to be generous towards others.
Enable me today
   to say something, or do something,
   that will make a difference
   to the discouraged, to the inexperienced, to the despairing.
Let no selfish concern with my own affairs
   shut me off from any today. Amen.

Reading

1   It is quite easy to found a community. There are always plenty of courageous
people who want to be heroes, are ready to sleep on the ground, to work hard
hours each day, to live in dilapidated houses. It's not hard to camp – anyone
can rough it for a time. So the problem is not in getting the community started
– there's always enough energy for take-off. The problem comes when we are
in orbit and going round and round the same circuit. The problem is in living
with brothers and sisters whom we have not chosen, but who have been given
to us, and in working ever more truthfully towards the goals of the community.

2 A community which is just an explosion of heroism is not a true community. True community implies a way of living and seeing reality; it implies above all *fidelity in the daily round*. And this is made up of simple things – getting meals, using and washing the dishes and using them again, going to meetings – as well as gifts, joy and celebration.

3 A community is only being created when its members accept that they are not going to achieve great things, that they are not going to be heroes, but simply live each day with new hope, like children, in wonderment as the sun rises and in thanksgiving as it sets. Community is only being created when they have recognised that human greatness is to accept our insignificance, our human condition and our earth, and to thank God for having put in a finite body the seeds of eternity which are visible in small and daily gestures of love and forgiveness. The beauty of humanity is in *this fidelity to the wonder of each day*.

37 Prefix Prayer   Frank Topping

1 Lord, I want to be an instrument of your peace.
   I sometimes wish I could do heroic things;
      be a saint; do something beautiful for you.
   But there is nothing extraordinary about me.
   I gaze at the great saints with awe
      and their very saintliness is frightening.

2 Yet, in my own experience, the instruments of your peace
      have never been very dramatic.
   Your peace has come to me
      through simple, common things:
      acts of kindness, gestures of love from people
      who have accidentally given me a glimpse of your love.

3 But perhaps I can only bear to see a glimpse of the love
      that embraces the world,
      the love that laughs, weeps, lives and dies
      with and for the whole of humanity.
   Perhaps a glimpse is all I can take.

4 Lord, let me reflect that light that *is* given to me.
   Let me recognise the love and the joy and the peace
      that *is* in my life,
      and to share it with whoever will receive it.

Personal Reflection

1   It is easy to love people who are far away.
    It is not always easy to love those who are close to us.
    It is easier to give a few pounds to relieve famine in Africa
    than to relieve the loneliness of someone living next door.
    In other words, it is easier to love at a distance,
    but not so easy to love at close quarters.

2   But does Christ really expect me to love
    that woman next door who never stops gossiping,
    that stupid fellow I have to work beside every day,
    that unfriendly bus conductor who never smiles,
    that shouting party member or social climber,
    that bad-tempered foreman,
    that neighbour's cheeky, spoiled brats?

3   Ah, if only they were in China or India, and they needed my help,
    I would be moved with pity and send them something.
    But these are right on my doorstep.

Prayer

Become flesh again in me, Lord.
Let your timeless and everlasting love
    live out each sunrise to sunset
    within the possibilities
    and the impossibilities
    of my own, very human life.
Help me to become
    Christ to my neighbour,
    food to the hungry,
    health to the sick,
    friend to the lonely,
    and freedom to the enslaved
    in all my daily living.

Personal Reflection

Drudgery is one of the finest touchstones of character there is. Drudgery is work that is very far removed from anything to do with the ideal – the utterly mean, grubby things; and when we come in contact with them we know instantly whether or not we are spiritually real. Read John 13; we see there the incarnate God doing the most desperate piece of drudgery, washing fishermen's feet, and he says – *"If I, then, your Lord and Master, have washed your feet, you also ought to wash one another's feet."* It requires the inspiration of God to go through drudgery with the light of God upon it. Some people do a certain thing, and the way in which they do it hallows that thing for ever afterwards. It may be the most commonplace thing, but after we have seen them do it, it becomes different. When the Lord does a thing through us, he always transfigures it. Our Lord took on our human flesh and transfigured it, and it has become for every saint the temple of the Holy Spirit.

(pause)

41 Blessing NH

God our Father, it is in you
　　that we live and move and have our being. Acts 17^{28}
Inspire us to live in such a way
　　that our choices each day
　　will lead us to live faithfully the present moment,
　　and transform the ordinariness of daily life
　　into something extraordinary.
Bless us this day and always. Amen.

In your presence
I am filled with wonder

Gathering in the Presence of God

NH   **42**

1 Lord, you tell each of us
  to love our neighbour
  as we love ourselves.

Mt 22³⁹

2 Sometimes we focus simply
  on aiming to do good to our neighbour,
  and forget how important it is
  to love ourselves.

3 Now, in your presence,
  as you look warmly at each one of us,
  lead us to be genuinely loving
  in the way we treat ourselves.

4 Lead us to see ourselves as you see us
  as we pause to remember
  that you are with us now.

(pause)

Reading

Edward Farrell   **43**

Prayer essentially is to become present
to oneself, to God, to all reality…

We are so caught up
with the events and the people in our lives
that we rarely take time
to consider our own selves
to be worth any time at all…

The closest reality to God
that one will ever experience
is oneself.

Each of us is an existence of God,
a presence of Christ,
a Sacrament of the Church,
a gift to the world.

44 Prayer

Terence Collins, FSC

1 Lord and God, great and mighty,
  in your presence
  I am filled with wonder!

2 I cannot fathom the greatness of your power
  or the depths of your wisdom.
 And yet I presume to praise you
  – a small speck in your creation.
 I seek to glorify you.

3 You have put in my heart
  this desire to praise you,
  this need to worship you.
 You have made me for yourself,
  and my heart will never be at ease
  until it rests in you.

4 You are beyond my knowledge,
  and yet I seek to praise you.
 I can never know you fully,
  yet I am moved to call on you
  by the Spirit
  that comes from the faith you have given me
  in the humanity of Jesus, your Son.

45 Personal Reflection

Peter van Breemen, SJ

It is fairly easy to believe in God's love in general, but it is very difficult to believe in God's love for me personally. Why me? There are very few people who can really accept themselves, accept acceptance. Indeed it is rare to meet a person who can cope with the problem, "Why me?" Self-acceptance can never be based on my own self, my own qualities. Such a foundation would collapse. Self-acceptance is an act of faith. When God loves me, I must accept myself as well. I cannot be more demanding than God, can I?

46 Psalm 139

NH

Lord, lover of life,
  you know the depths of my innermost self,
  and you understand me.
 You protect me on every side,
  shielding me from all harm.
 When you put me together carefully
  in my mother's womb,

you knew all about me.
I thank you for the wonder of myself
and I stand in awe
at all that you have made.
Guide me in your ways.

Reading

Peter van Breemen, SJ **47**

1 One of the deepest needs of the human heart is the need to be appreciated. Every human being craves to be accepted for what he is... When I am not accepted, then something in me is broken. A baby who is not accepted is ruined at the roots of his existence... Acceptance means that the people with whom I live give me a feeling of self-respect, a feeling that I am worthwhile. They are happy that I am who I am. Acceptance means that I am happy to be myself... I do not have to be the person I am not. Neither am I locked in by my past or present. Rather, I am given room to unfold, to outgrow the mistakes of the past...

2 When a person is appreciated for what he **does**, he is not unique; someone else can do the work, perhaps even better than he. But when a person is loved for what he **is**, then he becomes a unique and irreplaceable personality. I need that acceptance in order to be myself. When I am not accepted, I am a nobody; I cannot come to fulfilment. An accepted person is a happy person because he is opened up, because he can grow...

3 I am accepted by God as I am – **as I am** – and not as I should be... He loves me with my ideals and disappointments, my sacrifices and my joys, my successes and my failures. God is himself the deepest Ground of my being. It is one thing to know I am accepted, and quite another thing to realise it. It is not enough to have but just once touched the love of God. There is more required to build one's life on God's love. It takes a long time to believe that I am accepted by God as I am.

Prayer

NH   **48**

We will be glad and rejoice, Lord,
    because of your constant love.
Your own hands shaped us and modelled us,
    and you have watched each breath with tender care.
We rejoice that your kindnesses are never exhausted
    but are renewed every morning:
    great is your faithfulness.
Fulfil our needs, we ask you, Lord,
    as lavishly as only you can,
    because we are not relying on our own good works
    but on your great mercy. Amen.

49 Blessing

Compassionate Lord,
    you brought sight to the blind
    and raised up all who were bowed down:
Bless us and those we love.

Powerful Lord,
    you calmed the storm
    and brought peace to those who were troubled:
Bless us and those we love.

Healing Lord,
    you asked: *"What do you want me to do for you?"*
Bless us and those we love.

The prayer, *'We will be glad and rejoice, Lord'* (48), includes references to:
Ps 31[7], Job 10[8,12], Lam 3[23], Phil 4[19], Dan 9[18]

The Good News
that God loves the unworthy

(Louis Evely)

Gathering in the Presence of God

NH   **50**

Lord, the Roman officer
    whose servant was ill
    sent you a message:
"I am not worthy to receive you,
    but only say the word
    and my servant will get better."
We, too, can say
    that we are not worthy, Lord,
    to have you with us
    – but isn't your message all along
    that you wish and choose
    to be with us?
We spend a moment reminding ourselves
    that you choose to be here with us now.

(pause)

Reading

Louis Evely   **51**

Christianity is the good news
that God loves the unworthy,
that he does not need us to be worthy
in order to love us.
And the consequence is vital:
you will behave like your God.

Let us pray together: **Our Father, who art in heaven...**

Personal Reflection

Cardinal Basil Hume   **52**

Always think of God as your lover. Therefore he wants to be with you, just as a lover always wants to be with the beloved. He wants your attention, as every lover wants the attention of the beloved. He wants to listen to you, as every lover wants to hear the voice of the beloved. If you turn to me and ask – "Are you in love with God?" – I would pause, hesitate and say, "I am not certain. But of one thing I *am* certain: that he is in love with me."

53 **Prayer**

1 May you be blessed for ever, Lord,
for not abandoning me when I abandoned you,
and for offering your hand of love
in my darkest, most lonely moments.

2 May you be blessed for ever, Lord,
for putting up with such a stubborn soul as mine,
and for loving me more than I love myself.

3 May you be blessed for ever, Lord,
for continuing to pour out your blessings upon me,
even though I respond so poorly,
and for drawing out the goodness in all people,
even including me.

4 May you be blessed for ever, Lord,
for repaying my sin with your love,
and for being constant and unchanging
amidst all the changes of the world.

5 May you be blessed for ever, Lord,
for your countless blessings on me
and on all your creatures.

54 **Reading**

Margaret Sonnenday

After struggling to choose an answer to the question of what is most precious in
my life, I believe I now see it clearly: most precious to me is the assurance of the
grace of God – and its availability! To me, this means:
– that God loves me when I least deserve to be loved;
– that God accepts me as I am (in so many ways unacceptable);
– that God forgives me, again and again, when I fall short of my commitments;
– that every day I have a chance – a fresh start – to try again.

It is this grace which gives me the courage (and endows me with some skill) to
attempt to do more than I am able to do, and to become more than I can ever
become. God's grace frees me to dare and to risk.

55 **Prayer**

Ephesians 2$^{4-10}$
(J B Phillips)

1 Even though we were dead in our sins
God was so rich in mercy
that he gave us the very life of Christ
– for it is, remember, by grace and not by achievement
that you are saved.

2   And he has lifted us right out of the old life
     to take our place with him in Christ
     in the heavens.

3   Thus he shows for all time
     the tremendous generosity
     of the grace and kindness
     he has expressed to us in Christ Jesus.

4   It was nothing you could or did achieve
     – it was God's gift to you.

5   No-one can pride themselves
     that they 'earned' the love of God.
     The fact is, that what we are,
     we owe to the Hand of God upon us.

6   We are born afresh in Christ,
     and born to do those good deeds
     which God planned for us to do.

     Glory be…

Personal Reflection   56

In his final sermon as Abbot of Ampleforth Abbey in Yorkshire, before leaving to
become Archbishop of Westminster, Cardinal Basil Hume said:

"It is good to feel small,
for I know that whatever I achieve
will be God's achievement, not mine."

Blessing   Jude 1$^{1-2}$ 57

     To all who have been called by God,
     who live in the love of God the Father
     and the protection of Jesus Christ:
     may God's mercy, peace and love
     be ours in full measure. Amen.

Jesus, the healer, is the Good Shepherd

Gathering in the Presence of God

58

As we gather together to pray, let us first remind ourselves that God is already with us, as we say together:

**Good Shepherd,
lead us to recognise
that you are already in our midst,
loving and caring.**

(pause)

Prayer

NH   59

Lord Jesus,
   we are your people,
   the sheep of your flock.
You care for us
   as a shepherd guards his own,
   lying in the gateway of the fold at night,
   shielding us from harm.
You know us through and through,
   looking for the lost,
   bringing back the stray,
   binding up our wounds,
   and building up the weak.
It is by name that you call us,
   and where you lead
   you invite us to follow.
Inspire us to trust you more
   and lead us now to springs of living water.

(pause)

Reading

Archbishop Desmond   60
Tutu

God is like the Good Shepherd who goes out looking for the lost sheep (cf Lk 15:4). We are misled by the religious pictures which depict Jesus as the Good Shepherd carrying a cuddly white lamb on his shoulder. No; a lamb will hardly stray from its mother. It is the troublesome, obstreperous sheep which is likely to go astray, going through the fence, having its wool torn and probably ending up in a ditch of dirty water. It is this dirty, smelly, riotous creature which the Good

Shepherd goes after, leaving the good, well-behaved ninety-nine sheep in the wilderness, and when he finds it, why, he carries it on his shoulder and calls his friends to celebrate with him.

61 Prayer

Frank Topping

1 Again and again,
    I am offered the strength and support
    of love that will never fail:
        "Even though I walk   Ps 23
        through the valley of the shadow of death,
        I will fear no evil, for you are with me."

2 With such a shepherd I should not want,
    and yet, time after time, I find myself distanced
    from the care and protection of the shepherd.
Like a startled and terrified lamb
    leaping blindly into ditches and gullies,
    I find myself not knowing where to run for safety:
    so fraught that even hearing and knowing the shepherd's voice
    I am too confused to know which way to turn.

3 Sometimes it's hard to imagine
    that I am known to you, Lord:
    that the Good Shepherd knows my name
    and sees my distress, knows my doubts, hears my questions;
    but sparrows fall and my heavenly Father knows.
The hairs on my head are numbered,
    and the Shepherd does know me, better than I know myself.

4 Good Shepherd, when the events of my life
    worry, disturb, or even frighten me,
    when anxiety makes it difficult to think straight,
    let me hear your voice.
Lead me beside the still waters of your peace.

5 Remind me
    that even in the presence
    of those I might call enemies,
    you are with me; your strength is available for me.
Good Shepherd, as I am known to you,
    be known to me in goodness and mercy
    throughout this day, and all the days of my life.

Reading

Jean Vanier 62

1 Jesus, the healer, is the good shepherd
   who teaches us to walk
   in the paths of the Beatitudes.
   As the healer calls us to heal,
      so the shepherd calls us forth
      to be shepherds.

2 The extraordinary role of the shepherd
      is to listen to the flock without fear,
      to understand their language,
      to give each according to his need,
      to be wounded when one of the flock is wounded,
      to be in anguish when one of them is in anguish,
      to seek out those who have gone astray
      and bring them back,
      to be firm when it is necessary to be firm…

3 It is when people are *not* taught
      to pray and to enter into the mystical movement of Christianity,
      when they are *not* "called forth" to experience real love,
      that they turn to other pastures
      which do not really nourish.

4 They turn away
      because they have not learned from their shepherd
      how to communicate with God,
      how to listen to the Spirit,
      how to discern the things which are of God
      and the things which are not…
   If there is no real pasture,
      people will die of depression, of starvation.
   They will die thirsting.

5 We must learn to grow in shepherdhood.
      This cannot be done without the grace of the Spirit.

Blessing

St Ethelwold 63

Lord Jesus, Good Shepherd,
   you laid down your life for the sheep:
   defend those for whom you shed your blood.
Feed the hungry, give drink to the thirsty, seek the lost,
   convert the wandering, bind up that which is broken.

WALK IN MY PRESENCE

Stretch out your hand from heaven
and touch the head of each one here.
May we feel the touch of your hand
and receive the joy of the Holy Spirit,
and live in your peace for evermore. Amen.

The prayer, 'Lord Jesus, Good Shepherd', is built around the texts of
Jn 10$^{1-21}$, Ps 100^3, Ez 34^{16}, Rev 7^{17}

In the hands of God

Gathering in the Presence of God

Martin Luther   **64**

Martin Luther wrote:

>*"Rest in the Lord;*
>*wait patiently for him.*
>*Be silent before God and let him mould you.*
>*Keep still, and he will mould you to the right shape."*

Let us pray together:

NH

> **Holy Spirit,**
> > **our intention as we gather**
> > **is to pray with one another.**
>
> **We ask you now to pray in us**
> > **and lead us to be at rest and at peace**
> > **in your presence.**
>
> **Come, Holy Spirit,**
> > **fill us and mould us**
> > **and lead us to pray: *"Abba, Father".***

(pause)

Prayer

Sheila Cassidy   **65**

> Lord of creation,
> > moulder of our fragile clay,
> > shape us in your image.
>
> Spin us round, if you must,
> > until we're dizzy.
>
> Hollow us out, if you must,
> > until we're empty
> > of all that is false and useless.
>
> Fill us daily with living water
> > that we may carry your life
> > to a world dying of thirst.

Reading

St Ignatius Loyola   **66**

There are very few people who realise what God would make of them if they abandoned themselves into his hands, and let themselves be formed by his grace. A thick and shapeless tree-trunk would never believe that it could become a statue, admired as a miracle of sculpture, and would never submit itself to the chisel of the sculptor, who sees by his genius, what he can make of it. If only people would let themselves be formed by the grace of God.

67 Personal Reflection

Pedro Arrupe, SJ

More than ever, I now find myself in the hands of God.
This is what I wanted all my life from my youth.
And this is still the one thing I want.
But now there is a difference:
the initiative is entirely with God.
It is indeed a profound spiritual experience
to know and feel myself so totally in his hands.

68 Prayer

Charles de Foucauld

Father, I abandon myself into your hands;
    do with me what you will.
Whatever you may do, I thank you:
    I am ready for all, I accept all.
Let only your will be done in me
    and in all your creatures
    – I wish no more than this, O Lord.
Into your hands I commend my spirit;
    I offer it to you with all the love of my heart,
    for I love you, Lord, and so need to give myself,
    to surrender myself into your hands without reserve
    and with boundless confidence,
    for you are my Father.

69 Personal Reflection

Martin Luther

I have held many things in my hands
and I have lost them all;
but whatever I have placed in God's hands,
that I still possess.

70 Prayer

Cardinal John Henry
Newman

1   Let us put ourselves into his hands,
        and not be startled though he leads us by a strange way.
    Let us be sure he will lead us right,
        that he will lead us to that which is, not indeed what *we* think best,
        not what is best for another, but what is best for us.
    We are all created for his glory – we are created to do his will.

2   I am created to do something or to be something
        for which no-one else is created;
    I have a place in God's counsels, in God's world, which no-one else has,
        whether I be rich or poor, despised or esteemed by others:
        God knows me and calls me by name.

3 God has created me to do him some definite service.
He has committed some work to me
which he has not committed to another.
I have my mission – I may never know it in this life,
but I shall be told it in the next.
Somehow I am necessary for his purposes;
I have a great part in his work.

4 I am a link in a chain, a bond of connection between persons.
He has not created me for nothing.
I shall do good, I shall do his work.

5 I shall be an angel of peace, a preacher of truth in my own place,
while not intending it,
if I do but keep his commandments, and serve him in my calling.
Therefore I will trust him.

6 Whatever, wherever I am, I can never be thrown away.
If I am in sickness, my sickness may serve him;
if I am in perplexity, my perplexity may serve him;
if I am in sorrow, my sorrow may serve him.
My sickness or perplexity or sorrow
may be necessary causes of some great end
which is quite beyond us.
He does nothing in vain;
he may prolong my life, he may shorten it;
he knows what he is about.

ALL   *Lord, I give myself to you; I trust you wholly.*
You are wiser than I
– more loving to me than I am to myself.
Fulfil your great purposes in me, whatever they may be.
Work in and through me.
I am born to serve you, to be yours.

Personal Reflection

Teilhard de Chardin, SJ **71**

God needs to hollow us out, to empty us
in order to make room for himself.

(pause)

May the God of Strength be with us,
holding us in strong-fingered hands,
and may we be a sacrament of his Strength
to those whose hands we hold.
May the blessing of God's Strength be upon us. Amen.

Gathering in the Presence of God

73

It makes all the difference to focus not on our love for God but on his love for us! As we gather to pray, let us remind ourselves that he is with us.

(cf 1 Jn 4^{10})

(pause)

Reading

Alfred Monnin 74

There was a simple peasant, a good father of a family, whose fervent piety was the joy of his priest's heart. Whether going to his work or returning from it, never did that good man pass the church-door without entering it to adore his Lord. He would leave his tools, his spade, hoe and pickaxe at the door, and remain for hours sitting or kneeling before the tabernacle. Father Vianney, who watched him with great delight, could never perceive the slightest movement of the lips. Being surprised at this circumstance, he said to him one day: "What do you say to our Lord in these long visits you pay him every day and many times a day?" "I say nothing to him," was the reply; "I look at him, and he looks at me."

He said nothing, he opened no book, he could not read; but he had eyes – eyes of the body and eyes of the soul – and he opened them, those of the soul especially, and fixed them on our Lord… There was an interchange of ineffable thought in those glances, which came and went between the heart of the servant and the heart of the Master.

Prayer

Denis Blackledge, SJ 75

1   Loving Lord,
        I once asked an old man
        to tell me something about prayer.
    He just looked at me smiling and said:
        "You pray by opening your eyes."

2   Loving Lord,
        praying is such an easy gift:
        as simple as breathing,
        as simple as opening our eyes,
        learning how to stop and look,
        learning how to gaze in wonderment and awe
        at the people-gifts around us,
        at the grandeur of creation around us.

3   There is no need for long courses:
        just a willingness
        to go about my being and doing each day
        with a growing ability for wide-eyed wonder,
        with the eyes of a five-year-old.

76   Reading

Pope John Paul II

1   With words simple and clear, Jesus outlined the requirements for admission to his heavenly Kingdom… The new spirit is to be gentle, generous, simple, and above all sincere; to avoid being arrogant, censorious, or self-seeking. The disciples of the new Kingdom must seek happiness even amidst poverty, deprivation, tears and oppression. To aim for the Kingdom requires a radical change in outlook, in mentality, in behaviour, in relations with others… In the Sermon on the Mount, Jesus… offers to all mankind a new way of life, a charter of Christian life.

2   How astonished those first listeners must have been at hearing these dramatic words of Christ – especially those who were poor in spirit, gentle, or afflicted, downtrodden and oppressed – to hear themselves proclaimed as eligible for entry into a heavenly Kingdom.

3   It is essential for us to understand that Jesus has a specific task in life for each and every one of us. Each one of us is hand-picked, called by name – by Jesus! There is no-one among us who does not have a divine vocation!… What God our Father is offering us through his Son is a new life as his real children, with Jesus for our brother; a pressing call to live, to love, to labour for the coming of his Kingdom. And, lest bewildered at what we must do, we hesitate, Jesus offers himself to be our guide, and says: *"Come, follow me!"*

77   Prayer

Matt 5$^{1-12}$
from the Sermon on the
Mount
NH

1   Happy are the poor in spirit
        – for the Kingdom of Heaven is theirs.

2   Happy are those who mourn
        – for they will be given courage and comfort.

3   Happy are the gentle and humble
        – for they shall have the earth as their heritage.

4   Happy are those who hunger and thirst
        for what is good and right
        – for they will be fully satisfied.

5   Happy are those who are merciful to others
    – for they will have mercy shown to them.

6   Happy are the utterly sincere
    – for they will see God.

7   Happy are those who promote peace
    – for they will be called God's children.

8   Happy are those who suffer persecution
    for the cause of goodness
    – for the Kingdom of Heaven is theirs.

    Glory be…

Reading
Edward Farrell   78

In the vision of Jesus, the poor reign with God, the sorrowing are consoled, the meek inherit the earth, the hungry and thirsty are filled, the single-hearted see God, the peacemakers are called the sons and daughters of God…

In the vision of Jesus, anyone who brings his or her gift to the altar, and recalls that a sister or a brother has a complaint, leaves the gift and goes first to be reconciled. In the vision of Jesus, you offer no resistance to injury. If anyone presses you for one mile, you go two. You love your enemy, and pray for those who persecute you. When the hour comes, you will be given what to say; the Spirit of your Father will be speaking in you. Your soul will find rest.

In the vision of Jesus, lepers are made whole, paralytics walk, the blind see, captives are set free, the poor have the gospel preached to them. In the vision of Jesus, you do not worry about your livelihood, what you are to eat or to drink; you ask and you receive. You have courage; your sins are forgiven. You know that you are loved. Because of your faith, because of your vision, it is done to you.

Blessing
Old Sarum Primer   79

God be in my head – and in my understanding.
God be in my eyes – and in my looking.
God be in my mouth – and in my speaking.
God be in my heart – and in my thinking.
God be at my end – and at my departing.

And may the grace of the Lord Jesus
be with us all. Amen.

Rev 22[21]

A look of love

Gathering in the Presence of God

NH   **80**
Mk 10$^{17-22}$

> Lord, we find in the Gospel
>> that a rich young man spoke to you,
>> asking what he needed to do
>> to live in God's kingdom.
>
> You looked steadily at him with love.
> As we are gathered now,
>> remembering that we are in your presence,
>> lead us to realise
>> that you look steadily at each of us
>> with great love.

(pause)

Prayer

Denis Blackledge, SJ   **81**

> Loving Lord,
>> to look with reverence and dignity
>> at another human being
>> confers grace and status,
>> just as a negative look can kill another
>> from the inside out.
>
> Teach us to look from the inside out,
>> so that something of the permanent look of love
>> that you have for each one of us
>> is reflected in our own gaze at others.

Reading

Ronald Rolheiser   **82**

1 To "*really see*" someone, especially someone who looks up to you,
>> is to give that person an important blessing.
>
> In a gaze of recognition, of understanding,
>> in an appreciative look, there is deep blessing.
>
> Often, it is not so important
>> that we say much to those for whom we are significant,
>> but it is very important that we see them…

2 Good kings and queens see their people;
>> good parents see their kids;
>> good teachers see their students;
>> good priests see their parishioners;

good coaches see their players;
good executives see their employees;
and, in really good restaurants,
the owner comes round to the tables and sees his or her customers
– and the customers are, without being able to explain why,
grateful that the owner took the time and pain to see them.
We are blessed by being seen…

3   Today the young are not being seen enough in this way.
Our youth are acting out in all kinds of ways
    as a means of getting our attention.
They want to, and they need to, be seen by us –
    parents, adults, teachers, priests, coaches, leaders.
They need our blessing.
They need to see, right in our eyes,
    the radical acceptance of their reality,
    and they need to read in our eyes the words:
        "You are my beloved child; in you I am well-pleased."   (cf Mk 1^{11})
Young people need our appreciative gaze;
    mostly they simply need our gaze.

4   One of the deepest hungers inside young people
        is the hunger for adult connection,
        the desire to be recognised, seen, by a significant adult.
They desperately need, and badly want,
        the blessing that comes from our gaze and presence.
They need for us to see them.
In the end, more than they want our words, they want our gaze…

83   Prayer   Michel Quoist

1   May my look, Lord,
        never be one of disappointment, disillusionment, despair;
        but may it know how to admire, contemplate, adore…
    May my eyes be penetrating enough
        to recognise your presence in the world,
        and may they never shut on the afflictions of others.

2   May my eyes be firm and steady,
        but may they also know how to soften in pity
        and be capable of tears.
    May my gaze not soil the one it touches.
    May it not disturb, but bring peace.

3 May it not sadden, but rather transmit joy.
   May it not attract in order to hold captive,
        but rather persuade others
        to rise above themselves to you…

4 Grant that my eyes may be startling
        because they are an encounter – an encounter with you.
   Grant that they be a call, a clarion call,
        that brings all the world to its doorstep,
        not because of me, Lord,
        but because you are to pass by.

5 So that my eyes may be all this, Lord,
        once more I give you my soul,
        I give you my body, I give you my eyes,
            that in looking at others
            it may be you who look at them
            and you who beckon.

Prayer   NH   84

1 Lord Jesus,
        it must have been with great love
        that you touched the heart of the rich young man:
        "you looked steadily at him and loved him".   Mk 10$^{17-22}$

2 You reminded him of the commandments,
        and I like to think that he replied sincerely
        when he said that he had kept them all from his earliest days.

3 When I tend to place my trust
        in the good deeds and intentions of my earlier days,
        remind me that it is always *'today'*
        that you look steadily at me and show me your love,
        and that it is *'today'* that you call me to follow you.

4 However faithful the young man was in living the commandments,
        "he turned away sad",
        trusting in the wealth of his own efforts
        rather than in your freely-given grace.
   There is a temptation
        to consider my wealth for the next life
        to accrue from a credit of good works at the end of each day!
   Do remind me
        that, important as good works are,
        they are a response to your grace, freely offered to me.

5 May your look of love transform my heart,
        and enable me to follow you more closely,
        that I may discover you to be my greatest wealth.
    Challenge me each day,
        continue to look steadily at me,
        and empower me with your Spirit.

6 I like to think that you often remembered the young man
        in the months ahead,
        and continued to love him greatly,
        and that you prayed for him in the silence of your heart.
    Remember me, too,
        and strengthen me with the conviction
        that you often pray for me
        at the right hand of our Father.

85 Blessing

NH

Lord, you look on us with love
    and call us to do the same
    to those to whom you send us.
Give us your vision
    and show us how to bring your blessing to others
    through our gaze and our presence.
Lead us to confirm for each person
    that you look on us all with great love.
Bless us, Lord, this day and always. Amen.

Gathering in the Presence of God

86

Lord, may the light that we see around us
remind us of your presence with us now:
you who are the Light of the World.

Jn 8^{12}, 9^5

(pause)

Prayer

Frank Topping   87

Lord, my eyes deceive me,
    my ears mislead me,
    my tongue lets me down,
    my thoughts are confused
    unless you are with me,
    unless you direct my looking, speaking, hearing,
    and all I think and say and am.
Lord, I ask you to enter that fraction of time
    before I think or speak,
    so that the knowledge of your presence
    may influence all I do.

Personal Reflection

Bede Griffiths   88

One day during my last term at school, I walked out alone in the evening, and heard the birds singing in that full chorus of song, which can only be heard at that time of the year at dawn or at sunset. I remember now the shock of surprise with which the sound broke on my ears. It seemed to me that I had never heard the birds singing before, and I wondered whether they sang like this all the year round, and I had never noticed it. As I walked on, I came upon some hawthorn trees in full bloom, and again I thought that I had never seen such a sight or experienced such sweetness before. If I had been brought suddenly among the trees of the Garden of Paradise and heard a choir of angels singing, I could not have been more surprised. I came then to where the sun was setting over the playing fields. A lark rose suddenly from the ground beside the tree where I was standing, and poured out its song above my head, and then sank, still singing, to its rest. Everything then grew still as the sunset faded and the veil of dusk began to cover the earth. I remember now the feeling of awe which came over me. I felt inclined to kneel on the ground, as though I had been standing in the presence of an angel; and I hardly dared to look on the face of the sky, because it seemed as though it was *but a veil before the face of God.*

89 Prayer
Frank Topping

Lord of life,
  there is no part of your creation
  that does not speak
  of the wonder of your being.
Lord of all created things,
  let me lift up my eyes just once this day.
May the passing problems of my waking hours
  be reduced to their proper size and place
  beneath the infinite sky.
May I know your presence,
  feel and breathe the breath of life
  which is your daily gift,
  and may I see
  in the beauty of the heavens
  the measure of your love.

90 Reading
Carlo Carretto

In order to understand the signs that you see, and perceive their significance, you must be small and humble of heart... It seems absurd, but it is precisely for this reason that many people remain outside the truth. *"Seeing they do not see, and hearing they do not hear..."* (Mt 13[13]). And God passes them by.

91 Prayer
Frank Topping

Lord, forgive me
  that so often I prefer blindness to sight;
  that I am afraid of seeing,
  because '*seeing*' might turn my life upside down,
  alter all my values,
  and change all my aims and ambitions.
To see through your eyes changes things
  – through your eyes I see
  that the only purpose is love,
  and the only life is love.
In spite of my hesitations
  and my reluctance to see the world through your eyes,
  Lord, heal me, that I may say:
  "One thing I know: I was blind, but now I see."

Jn 9[25]

92 Personal Reflection
Helen Keller

We differ, blind and seeing, one from another – not in our senses, but in the use we make of them, in the imagination and courage with which we seek wisdom beyond our senses... I have walked with people whose eyes are full of light, but who see nothing in wood, sea or sky, nothing in the city streets, nothing in books. What a witless masquerade is this seeing! It were better far to sail for ever in the night of blindness, with sense and feeling and mind, than to be thus content with the mere act of seeing. They have the sunset, the morning skies, the purple of distant hills – yet their souls voyage through this enchanted world with a barren stare.

Prayer NH 93

Today and always, Lord,
   you smile on me
   and embrace me with your love,
   walking by my side
   from the rising of the sun to its setting.
Open my eyes
   to the wonder of all that is around me
   and to the people who are part of my life each day.
Empower me with your Spirit
   and warm my heart
   so that I may love tenderly and act justly,
   drawing closer to you
   and to my brothers and sisters.
Inspire me each day
   that I may grow in faithfulness
   and walk humbly
   with you, our God. Amen.

(cf Lk 24, Ps 113, Mic 6)

Intercessions 94

Let us pray for all who have asked us to pray for them, for all who need our prayer, and for those we wish to remember before God…

Our Father…

Blessing A Celtic Blessing 95

May the God of gentleness
be with us,
caressing us with sunlight and rain and wind.
May his tenderness shine through us
to warm all those who are hurt and lonely.
May the blessing of gentleness
be upon us. Amen.

Gathering in the Presence of God

Donal Neary, SJ   **96**

Thank you, Lord,
    because I can recognise you
    in the beauty of nature,
    the smile of a child,
    the sympathy of a friend.
That's how I can see your face,
    hear your voice,
    feel your hand,
    sense your presence.

(pause)

Personal Reflection

NH   **97**

On behalf of the people, Moses climbed Mount Sinai and approached the Lord. God agreed a covenant-relationship with his people, and set out *the Law* in carved letters on two stone tablets. God's grandeur shone around and had such an effect that it was reflected in the face of Moses. On returning to the people, Moses had to wear a veil over his face, lest the reflection of God's glory dazzled them. The tablets of stone seemed to form a focus of God's presence, and the *Ark of the Covenant* was later designed to hold those tablets of stone, marking God's presence on earth. A place of rest was found for the *Ark of the Covenant* when King Solomon built his Temple some 300 years later. A large veil, or curtain, then separated the *Holy of Holies* – the place of the *Ark of the Covenant* – from the people.

Psalm 42²⁻³

98

Like the deer that yearns
for running streams,
so my soul is yearning
for you, my God.

My soul is thirsting for God,
the God of my life.
When can I enter and see
the face of God?

Glory be...

99 Personal Reflection

NH

At the death of Jesus the veil in the Temple was torn in two, perhaps conveying that the focus of God's presence was no longer restricted only to the ritually-pure priests who were allowed beyond that Temple veil. Instead, in Jesus – the perfect High Priest – God is fully accessible and present to us all. We can meet God face-to-face! Unlike Moses who had to wear a veil over his face, all of us now *'reflect like mirrors the brightness of the Lord with uncovered faces. By the Spirit, we are transfigured in ever-increasing splendour into that very image that we reflect!… God who said, "Let there be light shining out of darkness" has shone in our hearts to radiate the light of the knowledge of God's glory, the glory shining in the face of Jesus.'*   (2 Cor 3^{18},4^6)

100 Prayer

Lucien Deiss

1   God of truth, you who said to us,
    "If today you hear my voice,
    harden not your hearts,"
        we pray to you this day.

2   You who speak to us
    through the marvels of creation,
    which you give us for our joy:
        Open our eyes that we may recognise therein
        the trace of your steps.

3   You who speak to us
    through today's happenings:
        Make us attentive, so as to discern your holy will
        in each of our joys and pains.

4   You who speak to us
    through our brothers and sisters:
        Help us to discover your face
        in the faces of those who surround us.

5   You who speak to us through your Son, the living Word,
    announced by the prophets
    and proclaimed by the evangelists,
    you who speak to us even in our silences:
        Give us the grace to open our hearts to your calls,
        to listen to them with joy,
        to follow them with love
        until the twilight of our lives,
        when we will arrive at that eternal *'today'*
        when we will see you face to face,
        forever and ever. Amen.

Personal Reflection

1 *"In each of us*
   the Father sees reflected the face of his Son;
   so we, too, should see Christ in each other."

Cardinal Basil Hume, OSB **101**

2 The musical of Victor Hugo's *'Les Misérables'*
   has these words in its Finale:

Victor Hugo **102**

   "To love another person
   is to touch the face of God."

(pause)

Prayer

NH
based on a prayer by
Victor Hugo **103**

We who weep come to you, Lord,
   because you always
   share our sorrow.
We who suffer come to you,
   knowing that you cure.
We who are afraid come to you,
   because you smile on us.
We share in your life
   because you share ours
   and so we know, God of love,
   that to love another person
   is, indeed, to touch your face.
May we live in your love forever. Amen.

Personal Reflection

104

It was in 1941, during the darkest days of the Second World War, that John Magee – a young pilot in the Royal Air Force – wrote this vivid poem about the spirit and adventure of flying, and he writes of putting out his hand and *'touching the face of God'*. Three months later, at the age of 19, he was killed in an air collision.

Oh! I have slipped the surly bonds of Earth
And danced the skies on laughter-silvered wings;
Sunward I've climbed, and joined the tumbling mirth
Of sun-split clouds – and done a hundred things
You have not dreamed of
– wheeled and soared and swung
High in the sunlit silence. Hov'ring there,
I've chased the shouting wind along, and flung
My eager craft through footless halls of air.

John Magee

Up, up the long, delirious burning blue
I've topped the wind-swept heights with easy grace,
Where never lark, or even eagle flew –
And, while with silent, lifting mind I've trod
The high untrespassed sanctity of space,
Put out my hand and touched the face of God.

(pause)

105 Blessing

cf Heb 1[3]

May Jesus,
who reflects the brightness of God's glory
and is the exact likeness of God's own being,
sustaining all things by his powerful word,
now give us his blessing and peace. Amen.

On 28 January 1986 the United States' Space Shuttle, '*Challenger*', exploded shortly after lift-off. In a subsequent speech to the people of the United States, President Ronald Reagan quoted from this poem (104) by John Magee.

Reflected glory

Gathering in the Presence of God

NH 106

Father, in all that you have made
    we see a reflection of your glory.
As your Spirit hovered over the waters of creation,
    breathe your Spirit into us now
    that he may renew our life
    and lead us to address you
    as *"Abba, dear Father"*.

(pause)

Reading

NH 107

In December 1968, the crew of Apollo 8 began their 480,000 mile journey, and became the first people to orbit the moon. The enterprise, of course, was built with the technological experience of many, and millions of people in many countries were able to see pictures from the moon, showing the earth reflecting the light of the sun. The astronauts referred to *"the good earth"* and then, on Christmas Eve, the navigator announced that the whole crew wished to convey a Christmas message to all. He read the opening poetic verses of the Book of Genesis.

Prayer

Genesis 1[1-19] 108

1   In the beginning, God created the heavens and the earth.
    Now the earth was a formless void,
        there was darkness over the deep,
        and God's Spirit hovered over the water.

2   God said, *"Let there be light"*, and there was light.
    God saw that the light was good,
        and God divided light from darkness.
    God called light *"day"*, and darkness he called *"night"*.
    Evening came and morning came: the first day.

3   God said, *"Let there be a vault in the heavens*
        to divide the waters in two."
    And so it was…
    Evening came and morning came: the second day.

4   God said, *"Let the waters under heaven*
        come together in a single mass,
        and let the dry land appear."

And so it was.
God called the dry land "*earth*",
    and the mass of waters "*seas*".
And God saw that it was good.

5   God said, "*Let the earth produce vegetation:*
     seed-bearing plants,
     and fruit trees bearing fruit with their seed inside."
   And so it was…
   God saw that it was good.
   Evening came and morning came: the third day.

6   God said, "*Let there be lights in the vault of heaven*
     to shine on the earth, to divide day from night,
     and let them indicate festivals, days and years."
   And so it was.
   God made the two great lights:
     the greater light to govern the day,
     the smaller light to govern the night,
     and the stars…
   God saw that it was good.
   Evening came and morning came: the fourth day…

   Glory be…

109 Personal Reflection NH

On Sunday 20 July 1969, Apollo 11 came to rest on the powdery surface of the moon. It was the first manned spacecraft to land there and, before they left the moon, astronauts Neil Armstrong and Buzz Aldrin placed a specially-prepared capsule on the surface, where it remains today. It contains a copy of Psalm 8.

110 Psalm 8 NH

1   Lord, our God and King,
    your greatness is seen throughout the earth.

2   When I gaze at the heavens
    which your fingers have formed,
    and look at the moon and the stars
    which you have set there,
    I realise how small we are
    in the majesty of your creation.

3   Yet you treasure us
    above all that you have made,

and you give us control
over all the works of your hand
– animals both wild and tame,
birds in the air,
and the creatures of the sea.

4   Lord, our God and King,
your greatness is seen throughout the earth.

Glory be…

Reading

St Gregory of Nyssa   **111**

Know to what extent the Creator has honoured you above all the rest of creation. The sky is not an image of God, nor is the moon, nor the sun, nor the beauty of the stars, nor anything of what can be seen in creation. You alone have been made the image of the reality that transcends all understanding, the likeness of imperishable beauty, the imprint of true divinity, the recipient of beatitude, the seal of the true light. When you turn to him, you become that which he is himself… There is nothing so great among beings that it can be compared with your greatness. God is able to measure the whole heavens with his span. The earth and the sea are enclosed in the hollow of his hand. And although he is so great and holds all creation in the palm of his hand, you are able to hold him: he dwells in you and moves within you without constraint, for he has said, *'I will live and move among them'* .

(2 Corinthians 6:16)

Prayer

The Astronauts' Prayer   **112**

Give us, O God, the vision
which can see your love in the world
in spite of human failure.
Give us the faith, the trust, and the goodness
in spite of our ignorance and weakness.
Give us the knowledge
that we may continue to pray
with understanding hearts,
and show us what each one of us can do
to set forth
the coming of the day of universal peace. Amen.

Blessing

NH   **113**

1   Lord our God,
time and again you have proclaimed
that what you have made
is good, is blest.
Lead us to respect all that is good around us.

2   Lead us to treasure each individual
        who comes into our lives,
        and have such respect and love
        for all of humanity
        that we sense that what is done to one person
        is done to all.

3   Look in our faces,
        and see there
        the image of Jesus, your Son,
        whom you sent among us
        because you love the world so much.

4   Bless us and all whom we cherish.
    Bless us this day and always. Amen.

Gathering in the Presence of God

NH 114

cf Mt 21[22]

Lord, you said
    that if we really believe,
    then whatever we ask for in prayer
    we will receive.
We ask first of all, Lord,
    that we may grow more aware
    that you are with us now.

(pause)

Psalm 104

NH 115

1 Lord our God, how great you are,
    and I give thanks to you.

2 You stretch out the heavens like a tent,
    with the sun to mark our days of work
    and the moon for our nights of rest.

3 With your fingers you formed the earth
    and wrapped it with the ocean like a cloak.
  The ships sail there,
    and beneath them glide the great sea creatures
    that you made to play with.

4 You pour down rain which the ground takes up.
  You set springs gushing forth in the valleys,
    and streams that flow between the mountains,
    bringing water to all that lives.

5 You make grass grow for the cattle
    and crops in abundance for our needs.
  You bring goodness to the trees,
    and in their branches the birds build their nests.
  Swarms of all living creatures are so many
    that they could never be counted.
  What variety you have created, Lord,
    arranging everything so wisely!

6 You send your Spirit, and all things have life.
Fill us with your Spirit, Lord,
    and give us new life,
    and renew the earth that you love.

Glory be…

116 Reading
Edward King

I will thank him for the pleasures given me through my senses, for the glory of the thunder, for the mystery of music, the singing of birds, and the laughter of children. I will thank him for the pleasures of seeing, for the delights through colour, for the awe of the sunset, the beauty of flowers, the smile of friendship and the look of love; for the changing beauty of the clouds, for the wild roses in the hedges, for the form and beauty of birds, for the leaves on the trees in spring and autumn, for the witness of the leafless trees through the winter, teaching us that death is sleep and not destruction, for the sweetness of flowers and the scent of hay. Truly, O Lord, *"the earth is full of thy riches!"* And yet, how much more I will thank and praise God for the strength of my body enabling me to work, for the refreshment of sleep, for my daily bread, for the days of painless health, for the gift of my mind and the gift of my conscience, for his loving guidance of my mind ever since it first began to think, and of my heart ever since it first began to love.

117 Prayer
Frank Topping

Lord, let me not be so removed
    from the rhythm of natural things
    that I fail to hear you
    speaking to me in the wind;
so cushioned by mechanical comforts
    that I fail to feel your power
    in the warmth of the sun;
so bedazzled by the brilliance of our inventions
    that I fail to see your light in a morning sky.
Lord, grant me the wisdom of the mind of an adult,
    but keep within me the heart of a child.

118 Prayer
Sirach 43[11-22,26-32]

1 See the rainbow and praise its Maker,
    so superbly beautiful in its splendour.
Across the sky it forms a glorious arc
    drawn by the hands of the Most High.

2 By his command he sends the snow,
    he speeds the lightning as he orders.

His treasuries open
     and the clouds fly out like birds.
In his great might he banks up the clouds,
     and shivers them into fragments of hail.

3 At sight of him the mountains rock,
       at the roar of his thunder the earth writhes in labour.
   At his will the south wind blows,
       or the storm from the north, and the whirlwind.

4 He sprinkles snow like birds alighting,
       it comes down like locusts settling.
   The eye marvels at the beauty of its whiteness,
       and the mind is amazed at its falling.
   Over the earth, like salt, he also pours frost
       which, when it freezes, bristles like thorns.

5 He swallows up the mountains and scorches the desert,
       like a fire he consumes the vegetation.
   But the mist heals everything in good time;
       after the heat, falls the reviving dew.
   Thanks to him all ends well,
       and all things hold together by means of his word.

6 He is the Great One, the awe-inspiring Lord,
       wonderful in his power.
   Who can glorify him as he deserves?
   Many mysteries remain even greater than these,
       for we have seen only a few of his works.

   Glory be…

Prayer   Iona Community   **119**

1 O God, your fertile earth is slowly being stripped of its riches:
   open our eyes to see.

2 O God, your living waters are slowly being choked with chemicals:
   open our eyes to see.

3 O God, your clear air is slowly being filled with pollutants:
   open our eyes to see.

4 O God, your creatures are slowly dying and your people are suffering:
   open our eyes to see.

5   God our Maker, so move us by the wonder of your creation,
    that we repent and care more deeply.

6   So move us to grieve the loss of life
    that we learn to cherish and protect your world.

120 Blessing

Numbers 6$^{24-26}$

May the Lord bless us and keep us.
May his face shine upon us.
May the Lord be gracious to us
and look upon us with kindness
and give us his peace. Amen.

Let all creation give praise

Gathering in the Presence of God

Lord Jesus,
    you promised to be with your people always.
Remind us now
    that you are with us
    as we gather to pray.
Breathe into us your Spirit
    that he may pray in us.

(pause)

Personal Reflection

And I have felt
A presence that disturbs me with the joy
Of elevated thoughts, a sense sublime
Of something far more deeply infused,
Whose dwelling is the light of setting suns,
And the round ocean and the living air,
And the blue sky, and in the mind of man:
A motion and a spirit, that impels
All thinking things, all objects of all thought,
And rolls through all things.

Prayer

If my lips could sing as many songs
as there are waves in the sea;
if my tongue could sing as many hymns
as there are ocean billows;
if my mouth filled the whole firmament with praise;
if my face shone like the sun and moon together;
if my hands were to hover in the sky like powerful eagles
and my feet ran across mountains as swiftly as the deer:
all that would not be enough
to pay you fitting tribute, O Lord, my God.

Personal Reflection

All you *big* things, bless the Lord:
    Mount Kilimanjaro and Lake Victoria,
    the Rift Valley and the Serengeti Plain,
    all eucalyptus and shady mango trees,

bless the Lord;
    praise and extol him for ever!
All you *tiny* things, bless the Lord:
    busy black ants and hopping fleas,
    wriggling tadpoles and mosquito larvae,
    flying locusts and water drops,
    pollen dust and tsetse flies,
      bless the Lord:
      praise and extol him for ever!

125 Prayer

Walter Rauschenbusch

1 God our Father,
    we thank you for this earth, our home;
    for the wide sky and the blessed sun,
    for the earth and the running water,
    for the everlasting hills and the never-resting winds,
    for trees and the common grass underfoot.

2 We thank you for our senses
    by which we hear the songs of birds,
    and see the splendour of the summer fields,
    and taste of the autumn fruits,
    and rejoice in the feel of the snow,
    and smell the breath of the spring.

3 Grant us hearts that are wide open to all this beauty;
    and save us from being so blind
    that we pass unseeing
    when even the common thornbush is aflame with your glory,
    O God, our Creator. Amen.

126 Personal Reflection

Elizabeth Barrett
Browning

Earth's crammed with heaven,
and every common bush afire with God:
but only he who sees
takes off his shoes;
the rest sit round it
and pluck blackberries.

(cf Ex 3^1-6)

127 Prayer

St Isidore of Seville

O God, great and wonderful,
    you have created the heavens,
    dwelling in their light and beauty.
You have made the earth,

WALK IN MY PRESENCE

revealing yourself in every flower that opens.
Let not my eyes be blind to you,
    nor my heart be dead to you,
    but teach me to praise you,
    even as the lark
    which offers her song at daybreak.

Personal Reflection Dom Helder Camara   **128**

Lord, isn't your creation wasteful?
Fruits never equal the seedling's abundance;
    springs scatter water;
    the sun gives out enormous light.
May your bounty teach me greatness of heart.
May your magnificence stop me being mean.
Seeing you a prodigal and open-handed giver,
    may I give unstintingly
    like a king's son,
    like your own Son. Amen.

Blessing NH   **129**

Father God,
    each part of your creation gives you praise
    by fulfilling what it was called to do.
Lead us now
    to live as the people you call us to be,
    and be gracious, Lord, in your gifts to us, Rom 12[3]
    especially in your blessing. Amen.

Gathering in the Presence of God NH 130

People are changed, Lord,
in the warmth of the sun.
So our lives are changed
in the radiance of your presence.
May your Spirit warm our hearts
and help us to realise
that you are, indeed,
with us now.

(pause)

Reading Helen Keller 131

Most of us take life for granted.
Only the deaf appreciate hearing;
only the blind realise the manifold blessings that lie in sight.
It is the same old story
of not being grateful for what we have until we lose it;
of not being conscious of health until we are ill.
But I, who am blind, can give one hint to those who see:
use your eyes as if tomorrow you would be stricken.
And the same method can be applied to the other senses:
hear the music of voices,
the song of the bird,
the mighty strains of an orchestra,
as if you would be stricken tomorrow.
Touch each object you want to touch
as if tomorrow your tactile sense would fail.
Smell the perfume of flowers,
taste with relish each morsel,
as if tomorrow you could never smell and taste again.
Make every sense glory
in the facets of the pleasure and beauty which the world reveals.
Thus, at last, you will *really see*,
and a new world of beauty will open up before you.

Prayer St Francis of Assisi 132

1 O Most High, Almighty, good Lord God,
to you belong praise, glory, honour and all blessing.

2 All praise be yours, my Lord, through all your creation
    and especially through our Brother Sun,
    who brings us the day
    and who brings us the night;
    he is strong, and shines magnificently.
  O Lord, we think of you when we look at him.

3 All praise be yours, my Lord, through Sister Moon
    and the stars
    which you have set clear and lovely in the heavens.

4 All praise be yours, my Lord, through Sister Water,
    who is very useful to us
    and humble, precious and very pure.

5 All praise be yours, my Lord, through Brother Fire,
    through whom you give us light in the darkness:
    he is bright and pleasant
    and very mighty and strong.

6 All praise be yours, my Lord, through Sister Earth, our Mother,
    who nourishes us and sustains us,
    bringing forth fruits and flowers of many colours,
    and vegetables to serve our needs.

7 All praise be yours, my Lord,
    through those who forgive for love of you;
    through those who endure sickness and tribulation,
    and who bear these things peaceably
    – you will grant them a crown.

8 All praise be yours, my Lord, through our Sister, Bodily Death,
    whom no-one can escape...
  Blessed are those
    whom death will find doing your holy will...

9 Praise and bless my Lord,
    and give thanks to him,
    and serve him with great humility.

133 Personal Reflection

If all the ocean was ink,
and if every blade of grass
was a quill with which to write;

A hymn of the Jewish
community

if the earth itself was parchment,
and if every person
started to write on it,
there would not be enough ink or pens
or parchment or people
to write fully
of God's love and greatness.

Prayer

F C Happold   **134**
Hymn of the Universe
T de Chardin

1   Let my mind be still,
      emptied of all thought of self,
      that in all quietness and humility
      I may bring before you, my Lord,
      the totality of the life of the earth.

2   On the paten of my heart
      I would place, O my Lord,
      the purposeful action of your people:
      their aspirations, their achievements, their work.
    Into my chalice I would pour their sorrows,
      and the failings and pain of every living being.

3   Into this oblation of the whole world
      I would gather first those closest to me,
      those whose lives
      are bound up with my own personal life,
      especially those I love,
      and those with whom I work.

4   With these, may I unite those more distant to me:
      the whole anonymous mass of mankind,
      scattered in every corner of the globe.
    And not only the living would I gather into this oblation,
      but also the dead.

5   And I would draw into it every form of life:
      animals and birds, reptiles and insects, trees and flowers,
      and all the kindly fruits of the earth.
    Let these, too, be laid upon this inner altar
      that they, too, may be offered to you.
    I present nothing less than everything to you, Lord.

ALL *May all life – past, present and future –*
be now elevated at the altar of my heart,
that in and through you, O Christ,
it may be presented to the Father.

135 Blessing

NH

We rejoice, Father,
in the beauty of all that you have made.
Bless us now
as we bring to you in offering
all that we are
and all that we value.
We ask this through Christ our Lord. Amen.

Touch our hearts

Gathering in the Presence of God

136

It has been said that
"only when the heart is not thumping
can the still, small voice of God be heard".
And so we pray:

Hubert Van Zeller, OSB

ALL **Lead us, Lord, to pause during this time**
and, in the quietness,
to appreciate that you are with us:
you who tell us to seek first God's kingdom.

NH

Mt 6³³

(pause)

Prayer

attributed to   137
Cardinal Cushing

1   Slow me down, Lord!
Ease the pounding of my heart
    by the quietening and calming of my mind.

2   Break the tensions of my nerves and muscles
        with the soothing music of the singing streams
        that live in my memory.
Give me, amid the confusion of the day,
        the calmness of the everlasting hills.

3   Steady my hurried pace
        with a vision of your eternal reach of time,
        and restore and heal me in the hours of sleep.

4   Teach me the art of appreciating what is ordinary:
        of slowing down to look at and become more aware
        of the beauty around me;
        to take time to be with others,
        to sit and enjoy music or a good book
        – to give myself time for myself.

5   Remind me each day of the fable of the hare and the tortoise,
        that I may know that the race is not always to the swift;
        that there is more to life than increasing its speed.

6   Let me look upwards into the branches of the towering trees
        and know that they grew great and strong
        because they grew slowly and well.

ALL   **Slow me down, Lord,**
        and inspire me to send my roots
        deep into the soil of life's enduring values.
      Slow me down, Lord,
        that I may grow true and well in your light.

138 Personal Reflection

Edward Farrell

Do you reverence yourself enough
to offer yourself the gift of time
with the One who calls you to dwell in his heart,
with the One who dwells within your own heart?

139 Reading

'Catechism of the
Catholic Church'

1   The spiritual tradition of the Church emphasises the *heart*, in the biblical sense of the depths of one's being, where the person decides for or against God. According to Scripture, it is the *heart* that prays. If our heart is far from God, the words of prayer are in vain.

2   The heart is the dwelling-place where I am, where I live; according to the Semitic or biblical expression, the heart is the place 'to which I withdraw'. The heart is our hidden centre, beyond the grasp of our reason and of others; only the Spirit of God can fathom the human heart and know it fully. The heart is the place of decision, deeper than our psychic drives. It is the place of truth, where we choose life or death. It is the place of encounter because, as image of God, we live in relation: it is the place of covenant.

140 Prayer

NH

1   Lord, it means so much to know
        that you are close to the broken-hearted
        and bind up all our wounds,
        that you proclaim liberty to captives
        and bring good news to the poor,
        that you are all tenderness and compassion
        and raise up all who are down-hearted.
      Send your Spirit into my heart
        to teach me to pray: 'Abba, Father'.

2   Open my heart
        to the promptings of your Spirit,
        and sow in me your Word.

Pour over me the water that is your Spirit,
    so that your Word may more readily grow in my heart
    and yield a great harvest.
I rejoice that my heart burns within
    when I recognise you walking beside me,
    explaining your Word to me.

3 You tell me not to let my heart
    become troubled or afraid.
I ask you not to let my heart grow hardened.
Instead, touch my heart with your Spirit
    and transform whatever you find to be like stone.
Give me wisdom and understanding
    and a warm heart
    whose love abounds like the seashore.

4 Remind me often
    how to set first my heart on your kingdom
    and what you require of me.
Then, as I seek you with all my heart,
    your promise is that I shall find you
    and know you to be always merciful and tender-hearted,
    slow to anger, loving and loyal.

ALL   ***Lord, you know my heart and my thoughts.***
You know everything in my heart
    and I can only be humble before you,
    as I ponder and treasure in my heart
    all that you have done for me.
I give thanks to you
    and offer you the gift of myself,
    asking you to make your home within me.

Intercessions

Frank Colquhoun   **141**

Heavenly Father,
    we bring to you in prayer
    people who are suffering in mind or spirit.
We remember especially those facing long and incurable illness;
    those cast down by the cares and sorrows of daily life;
    those who have lost their faith, and for whom the future is dark.
In your mercy maintain their courage,
    lift their burdens
    and renew their faith,
    that they may find in you
    their strength, their comfort and their peace. Amen.

142 Blessing   (cf Sir 50$^{22-24}$)

May the God of all
now bless us
and grant us cheerful hearts,
peace in our day,
and his mercy at all times. Amen.

The prayer (140) – *"Lord, it means so much to know"* – makes reference to Scripture:
Paragraph 1: Ps 34^{18}; Ps 147^3; Is 61$^{1-2}$, Lk 4$^{16-19}$; Joel 2^{13}; Lk 1^{51}; Gal 4^6
Paragraph 2: Lk 8^4; Ez 36^{25}; Lk 8^{15}; Lk 24^{32}
Paragraph 3: Jn 14^{27}; Ps 95^8; 2 Chron 34^{27}; Ez 11^{19}; 1 Kings 5^9
Paragraph 4: Mt 6^{33}; Jer 29^{13}; Deut 4^{29}; Ps 86^{15}
Paragraph 5: Ps 139^{23}; Rom 8^{27}; 2 Chron 34^{27}; Lk 2^{19}; 1 Chron 29^{17}; Jn 15^4

Gathering in the Presence of God NH 143

God our Father,
> gathered here in love, as we are,
> we rejoice that we live in you
> and you live in us.
Touch our hearts and minds
> as we start our prayer
> by reminding ourselves that you are with us.

(pause)

Personal Reflection NH 144

Lord Jesus,
when I become particularly conscious
of difficulties and limitations and worries,
when life seems to crowd in on me
and I become more conscious of 'failures',
convince me in my heart
that *"love never fails"*   1 Cor 13[8]
– that there is 'success'
whenever people love.

Lead me to grow in the faith deep-down
that you love me today – as I am –
in the reality of my life this day,
and then, living in your perfect love,
any fears and anxieties
will be cast away,   1 Jn 4[18]
and I will bear your fruit in plenty. Amen. Jn 18[5,9]

Prayer 1 Corinthians 13[1-7] 145

1 I may be able
> to speak the languages of people and even of angels,
> but if I have no love,
> my speech is no more
> than a noisy gong or a clanging bell.

2 I may have the gift of inspired preaching;
> I may have all knowledge and understand all secrets;

I may have all the faith needed to move mountains
  – but if I have no love, I am nothing.

3 I may give away everything I have,
    and even give up my body to be burnt
    – but if I have no love, this does me no good.

4 Love is patient and kind;
    it is not jealous or conceited or proud.
  Love is not ill-mannered or selfish or irritable.

5 Love does not keep a record of wrongs.
  Love is not happy with evil,
    but is happy with the truth.

6 Love never gives up;
    and its faith, hope, and patience never fail.

  Glory be…

146 Personal Reflection

Dorothy Day

Your love for God is only as great
as the love you have for the person you love least.

147 Prayer

Richard Harries

Help me, Lord, to be more like you:
  to draw a circle that includes rather than excludes.
Give me a genuine love for others,
  both those I like, and those I don't like.
Help me to overcome my fears and prejudices
  and to see your image in all. Amen.

148 Reading

Mother Teresa

We will never know just how much good a simple smile can do. We tell people how kind, forgiving and understanding God is, but are we the living proof? Can they really see this kindness, this forgiveness, this understanding, alive in us?

Be kind and merciful. Let no-one ever come to you without leaving better and happier. Be the living expression of God's kindness – kindness in your face, kindness in your eyes, kindness in your smile, kindness in your warm greeting. To children, to the poor, to all who suffer and are lonely, always give a happy smile. Give them not only your care, but also your heart. Because of God's goodness and love, every moment of our life can be the beginning of great things. Be open, ready to receive, and you will find him everywhere. Every work of love brings a person face-to-face with God.

Personal Reflection

Thank you, God,
for making me like I am.
I don't mind having Down's Syndrome.

Thank you for my family,
who love and spoil me.

Thank you for helping me
to beat most people at Nintendo,
especially Dad!

Thank you
for all the exciting things I do,
like going to the cinema, theatre,
concerts, Alton Towers and McDonalds.

Please help all people with handicaps
to be as happy as me. Amen.

Prayer

God our Father,
    the qualities I see lived out so well in some people
    are a reflection of your own goodness,
    and I know
    that I have much to learn from others
    who reflect your image and likeness
    in different ways than I do.
Inspire me
    to respect others fully as my equals,
    seeing and loving in them
    what you see and love in them. Amen.

Intercessions

Let us pray in silence for those whose
"little, nameless, unremembered acts
of kindness and love
...have had no trivial influence" on us...

(pause)

To the God of love we give thanks
for all whose lives have touched ours
with his love and compassion.

May God now bless us:
the Father, who so loved the world that he sent Jesus to us;
and the Son, whose love never ends;
and the Holy Spirit, who empowers us to love. Amen.

Gathering in the Presence of God

153

> Knowing that the Lord Jesus is present
> wherever his sisters and brothers are,
> let us ask him
> to make us more aware of his presence with us now

ALL   **and let us adore him.**

(pause)

Prayer

Frank Topping   154

> Lord, you have always taken the initiative.
> You did not delegate others
>   to visit the sick, or to comfort the sorrowful.
> You came into our lives
>   and healed by listening, talking, touching.
> You could not resist
>   the crisis of the lonely and the troubled;
>   you gave not only time, but your last breath.
> Lord, help me to respond generously to others.
> As you have time for me, may I have time for others.

Meditation

Matthew 25$^{31-45}$ 155

Narrator   When the Son of Man comes as King,
>   and all his angels with him,
>   he will sit on his royal throne,
>   and the people of all the nations will be gathered before him.
>   Then he will divide them into two groups,
>   just as a shepherd separates the sheep from the goats.
>   He will put the righteous people on his right,
>   and the others on his left.
>   Then the King will say to the people on his right:

1   *"Come, you that are blessed by my Father!*
> *Come and possess the kingdom*
>   *which has been prepared for you*
>   *even since the creation of the world.*
> *I was hungry and you fed me,*
>   *thirsty and you gave me a drink;*
> *I was a stranger and you received me in your homes,*

naked and you clothed me;
I was sick and you took care of me,
in prison and you visited me."

Narrator   The righteous will then answer him:

2   *"When, Lord, did we ever see you hungry and feed you,*
or thirsty and give you a drink?
When did we ever see you a stranger,
and welcome you in our homes,
or naked and clothe you?
When did we ever see you sick or in prison, and visit you?"

Narrator   The King will reply:

3   *"I tell you, whenever you did this*
for one of the least important
of these brothers and sisters of mine,
you did it for me!"

Narrator   Then he will say to those on his left:

4   *"Away from me, you that are under God's curse!*
Away to the eternal fire
which has been prepared for the Devil and his angels!
I was hungry but you would not feed me,
thirsty but you would not give me a drink;
I was a stranger but you would not welcome me in your homes,
naked but you would not clothe me;
I was sick and in prison, but you would not take care of me."

Narrator   Then they will answer him:

5   *"When, Lord, did we ever see you hungry or thirsty,*
or a stranger, or naked, or sick, or in prison,
and would not help you?"

Narrator   The King will reply:

6   *"I tell you,*
whenever you refused to help
one of these least important ones,
you refused to help me."

Reading

1 This is one of the most vivid parables which Jesus ever spoke, and the lesson of it is crystal clear. The lesson is this – that God will judge us in accordance with our reaction to human need. God's judgement does not depend on the knowledge we have amassed, or the fame that we have acquired, or the fortune that we have gained, but on the help that we have given. But there are certain things which this parable teaches us about the help which we must give.

2 It must be help in simple things. The things which Jesus picks out – giving a hungry man a meal, or a thirsty man a drink, welcoming a stranger, cheering the sick, visiting the prisoner – are things which anyone can do. It is not a question of giving away thousands of pounds, or of writing our names in the annals of history; it is a case of giving simple, human help to the people we meet every day. There never was a parable which so opened the way to glory to the simplest people.

3 It must be help which is quite uncalculating. Those who helped did not think that they were helping Christ, and thus piling up eternal merit; they helped because they could not stop themselves helping. It was the natural, instinctive, quite uncalculating reaction of the loving heart. Whereas, on the other hand, the whole attitude of those who failed to help was: *"If we had known it was **you**, we would gladly have helped; but we thought it was only some common person who was not worth helping."* It is still true that there are those who will help if they are given praise and thanks and publicity; but to help like that is not to help, it is simply to pander to self-esteem. Such help is not generosity; it is simply disguised selfishness. The help which wins the approval of God is the help which is given for nothing but the sake of helping.

Prayer

Lord, you tell us
　　that what we do to the very least
　　we do to you,
　　and that we are blessed by your Father.

Inspire us to touch hearts
　　by building up and renewing,
　　by welcoming people and restoring dignity,
　　by encouraging the weak
　　and lightening burdens.

Lead us to be generous
　　and not sit in judgement on others,
　　but to love one another as you love us. Amen.

158 Blessing

source unknown

1 May God bless us with discomfort
   at easy answers, half truths and superficial relationships,
   so that we will live deep within our hearts.

2 May God bless us with anger
   at injustice, oppression and exploitation of people,
   so that we will work for justice, equality and peace.

3 May God bless us with tears to shed
   for those who suffer from pain, rejection, starvation and war,
   so that we will reach out our hand to comfort them
   and change their pain into joy.

4 And may God bless us
   with the foolishness to think
   we can make a difference in the world,
   so that we will do the things
   which others tell us cannot be done. Amen.

Gathering in the Presence of God

Carlo Carretto   **159**

As our religious experience grows, we begin to realise that we meet God not only in the big events of our lives, but in all the events – however small and insignificant. God is never absent from our lives. He cannot be, because *'in him we live, and move, and exist'* (Acts 17:28).

And so let us remember that we are in the Presence of God
ALL   *and let us adore him*.

(pause)

Meditation

NH   **160**
reflecting on
Matthew 25$^{31\text{-}46}$ (a)

1   I was hungry for a generous word
        – and you smiled and talked warmly.
    I was hungry for a gesture of kindness
        – and you went beyond what I had hoped for.
    I was hungry for genuine understanding
        – and you heard beyond my words.

2   I was thirsty for life and vitality
        – and you helped me to grow.
    I was thirsty for encouragement
        – and you affirmed me and built me up.
    I was thirsty for moral support
        – and, willingly, you shared my cup of suffering.

3   I was a stranger to genuine welcome
        – and you gave me your full attention.
    I felt lonely
        – and you blessed me with your presence.
    I was a stranger to care and appreciation
        – and you treated me with courtesy and respect.

Reading

James 2$^{14\text{-}20,22}$ **161**

What use is it for someone to say they *"have faith"* if their actions do not correspond with it? If someone has no clothes to wear, and nothing to eat, and one of you says: *"Good luck to you; I hope you'll keep warm and find enough to eat,"* and yet give them nothing to meet their physical needs, what on earth is the good of that? Yet that is exactly what a bare faith – without a corresponding life – is like: useless and dead.

If we only *"have faith"* someone could easily challenge us by saying: *"You say that you have faith and that I have merely actions. Well, all you can do is to show me a faith without corresponding actions, but I can show you by my actions that I have faith as well."*

To anyone who thinks that faith by itself is enough, I feel inclined to say: *"So you believe that there is one God? That's fine; so do all the devils in hell!"* Can't you see far enough to realise that faith without the right actions is dead and useless? Faith and actions are partners.

162 Meditation

NH

reflecting on

Matthew 25[31-46] (b)

1 I was naked
because my dignity and self-respect were undermined
    – but you remained constant and faithful.
I was stripped of my good name
through rumours that were untrue
    – but you spoke up for me.
I felt diminished and vulnerable
    – but you restored my confidence and faith.

2 I was sick and tired and downcast
    – but you brought healing into my life.
I was anxious about my future
    – but you lifted my spirits, and your love cast out my fear.
I felt overburdened
    – but you shared my difficulties
    and helped me to carry my cross.

3 I felt imprisoned
by those who judged and sentenced me
    – but you accepted me for who I am.
I felt entrapped by circumstances,
    – but you showed me
    that I have control over my own life.
I was imprisoned by hurts and anguish
    – but you helped to ease the pain.

163 Prayer

Pope John Paul II

1 To you,
Creator of nature and humanity,
of truth and beauty, I pray:

2 Hear my voice,
for it is the voice

of the victims of all wars and violence
among individuals and nations.

3   Hear my voice,
    for it is the voice of all children who suffer and will suffer
    when people put their faith in weapons and war.

4   Hear my voice
    when I beg you to instil
    into the hearts of all human beings
    the vision of peace,
    the strength of justice
    and the joy of fellowship.

5   Hear my voice,
    for I speak for the multitudes
    in every country and in every period of history
    who do not want war
    and are ready to walk the road of peace.

6   Hear my voice
    and grant insight and strength
    so that we may always respond
    to hatred with love,
    to injustice with total dedication to justice,
    to need with the sharing of self,
    to war with peace.

7   O God, hear my voice,
    and grant to the world your everlasting peace. Amen.

Blessing

cf 2 Thess 1[11-12]   **164**

May God, by his power,
    fulfil every good intention,
    and complete all that we have been doing through faith.
And may the grace of our God
    and of the Lord Jesus Christ
    remain with us. Amen.

"Let justice flow like water, and integrity like an unfailing stream"

A22

(Amos 5:24)

Gathering in the Presence of God

NH   **165**

Father God,
>you look on us
>and on all our sisters and brothers
>with great love.

Touch our hearts anew
>that we may be alive with your Spirit
>and grow more aware
>that you are in our midst.

(pause)

Prayer

NH   **166**

1 God our Father, you so loved the world
>that you sent Jesus, your Son,
>to share our humanity and live fully as one of us.

2 We give you thanks
>for the talents you have given to mankind,
>and for the blessings received
>through those who use their gifts well.

3 We think of the beauty of the world
>which you proclaimed to be good,
>but we are also conscious of our misuse
>of what you have given to us:
>– from the ore in the ground
> we fashion bullets and weapons;
>– from the oil under the sea
> we derive explosives;
>– from the atoms of existence
> we produce bombs of mass destruction;
>– from living organisms
> we make weapons for biological warfare.

4 Our governments spend money in our name
>maintaining 'butter mountains' and 'wine lakes',
>and we subsidise farmers to 'set aside' land

so that less food is produced,
even though our brothers and sisters
die each day from hunger.

5   On our paper money
we print the images of famous people,
yet often do not treasure and uphold
the dignity of others who share our common humanity
and are made in your image and likeness.

6   Open our hearts to be influenced for good,
and inspire us to touch the hearts of others.
Enable us to change the things that contradict your love,
and may all your people
work and grow together as brothers and sisters
and further your kingdom on earth. Amen.

167 **Prayer**

Amnesty International

Lord Jesus, you experienced in person
torture and death
as a prisoner of conscience.
You were beaten and flogged
and sentenced to an agonising death,
though you had done no wrong.
Be now with prisoners of conscience throughout the world.
Be with them in their fear and loneliness,
in the agony of physical and mental torture,
and in the face of execution and death.
Stretch out your hands in power to break their chains.
Be merciful to the oppressor and the torturer,
and place a new heart within them.
Forgive all injustice in our lives,
and transform us to be instruments of your peace
for, by your wounds, we are healed.

168 **Prayer**

Terry Waite

O Lord:
in a world where many are lonely,
we thank you for our friendships.

In a world where many are captive,
we thank you for our freedom.

In a world where many are hungry,
we thank you for your provision.

We pray that you will
enlarge our sympathy,
deepen our compassion,
and give us grateful hearts,
in Christ's name.

Prayer NH   169

1   Lord, it's good to be actively concerned
     about the abuse of human rights elsewhere,
     but I must not lose sight
     of the mis-treatment of others closer to me.

2   I readily condemn slavery,
     but help me to liberate those I know
     who are overburdened.
  I condemn torture,
     but alert me when I am tempted
     to use cruel words and actions.
  In particular, Lord,
     point out to me my own failings.

3   Lead me always to respect each individual
     and grow in appreciation
     that those who think differently from me
     can hold equally valid views.
  Enlighten me
     so that I do not jump to conclusions about people,
     or be judgmental.

4   Lord, help me – help all of us –
     to grow in respect for all people.

Blessing NH   170

God our Father,
     we can think of people in many situations today
     who need your blessing.
Bless them and bless us
     and lead us all
     to be instruments of your peace
     and credible witnesses of your love
     in our world that you love so much. Amen.

"Act justly, love tenderly, and walk humbly with your God"

Gathering in the Presence of God

NH   171

1   Lord, open our eyes
     – that we may discover you in our midst.

2   Lord, open our hearts
     – that we may know your love.

3   Lord, open our lips
     – that we may speak your words.

4   Lord, open our hands
     – that we may receive your gifts
     and more readily share of ourselves
     with those to whom you send us.

(pause)

Prayer

NH   172

We ask you, Lord, to challenge us,
     especially when we become too set in our ways.
Inspire us
     to review our priorities and values,
     so that our attitude may be
     to give generously, without counting the cost.
Open our eyes and hearts to all people,
     and particularly to those
     who are vulnerable or marginalised,
     or who can do nothing for us in return.
Lead us to act justly, love tenderly,
     and walk humbly with you, our God. Amen.

Personal Reflection

173

Saint Ambrose was born about the year 339. He wrote:

"It is not from your own possessions
     that you are bestowing gifts on the poor:
     you are but restoring to them
     what is theirs by right

St Ambrose

– for what was given to everyone
for the use of all
you have taken for your exclusive use.
The earth belongs – not to the rich
– but to everyone.
So, far from giving lavishly,
you are only paying part of your debt."

174 Prayer

Annabel Shilson-Thomas

1 Compassionate God,
    open our hearts
    that we may feel the breath and play of your Spirit.

2 Unclench our hands
    that we may reach out to one another
    in openness and generosity.

3 Free our lips
    that we may speak
    for those whose voices are not heard.

4 Unblock our ears
    to hear the cries of the broken-hearted.

5 Open our eyes
    to see Christ in friend and stranger,
    that in sharing our love and our pain,
    our poverty and our prosperity,
    we may move towards that peace and justice
    which come from you,
    and so be bearers of divine reconciliation. Amen.

175 Personal Reflection

Saint Basil (329-379) wrote:

"The food you have stored away
    belongs to the hungry.
The unworn garment in your wardrobe
    belongs to the naked.
The gold you have hidden away
    belongs to the poor."

Saint Basil

Prayer

Julia Esquivel 176

1   Give us, Lord God, a vision of our world
        as your love would make it:
        – a world where the weak are protected,
        and none go hungry or poor;
        – a world where the benefits of civilised life are shared,
        and everyone can enjoy them;

2   – a world where different races, nations and cultures
        live in tolerance and mutual respect;
        – a world where peace is built with justice,
        and justice is guided by love;
        and give us the inspiration and courage to build it,
        through Jesus Christ our Lord.

3   Let your kingdom come
        which abolishes all that destroys life in the world:
        your kingdom which eradicates within people
        all that makes them live less than humanly.

4   Let your kingdom come:
        your kingdom which is freedom and love,
        which is sisterhood and brotherhood,
        which is righteousness and life,
        which is truth and justice. Amen.

Personal Reflection

Pope John Paul II 177

*"The poor of the world
    are your brothers and sisters in Christ.
You must never be content
    to leave them just the crumbs from the feast.
You must give of your substance
    and not just of abundance,
    in order to help them.
And you must treat them as guests at your family table."*

Dom Helder Camara 178

*"When I give food to the poor,
    they call me a saint.
When I ask why the poor have no food,
    they call me a communist."*

179 Blessing

    We stand before you, Father,
        in need of your mercy and kindness.
    Be as generous to us
        as we are to others,
        and give to all of us, we pray,
        the fullness of your blessing. Amen.

Gathering in the Presence of God

NH   **180**

Betrayed and condemned, Lord,
    abandoned and tortured,
    your slow execution was between two thieves:
    'in the midst of them'.   Jn 19[18]
We are reminded
    that you came to dwell among us,
    'in the midst' of people,   Jn 1[14]
    and you have been called *'God-is-with-us'.*   Mt 1[23]
As we gather to pray
    we ask you to remind us, loving Lord,
    that you are already in our midst.

(pause)

Reading of a Prayer

NH   **181**

1 Father,
    you have made all people in your own likeness
    and you love all that you have made.

2 Your Son was born a member of a Jewish family,
    was recognised by wise men from the east,
    and rejoiced in the faith of a Roman soldier and a Syrian woman.
    He praised Samaritans for their attitude and good works,
    welcomed the Greeks who searched for him,
    and was helped to carry his cross by an African.

3 May our human family not become separated from you
    by building barriers of race and colour,
    of class and creed.

4 Inspire us to recognise
    that we are all made in your image and likeness,
    so that we may grow in appreciation of all people,
    and encourage each other to grow in pride
    in who we are and who we are called to be.

5 May we recognise your Son in our midst,
    and live truly as brothers and sisters. Amen.

182 Prayer

Caryl Micklem

Lord,
    strengthen the hands of those who work
    to draw together
    people of different races.
May the children who play together
    remain friendly as they grow older.
May students enter deeply
    into each other's worlds.
May those who live as neighbours
    or work together
    strive to create truly human bonds.

183 Reading

Micah 4[1-5]

1 In the days to come,
    the mountain of the Temple of Yahweh
    will be put on the top of the mountains
    and be lifted higher than the hills.
  The peoples will stream to it;
    nations without number will come to it,
    and they will say:

2 "Come let us go up to the mountain of Yahweh,
    to the Temple of the God of Jacob,
    so that he may teach us his ways
    and we may walk in his paths;
    since from Zion the Law will go out,
    and the oracle of Yahweh from Jerusalem."

3 He will wield authority over many peoples
    and arbitrate for mighty nations;
    they will hammer their swords into ploughshares,
    their spears into sickles.
  Nation will not lift up sword against nation,
    there will be no more training for war.
  Each man will sit under his vine and his fig tree,
    with no one to trouble him.

184 Prayer of Peace

Pope Paul VI

1 Lord God of peace,
  we thank you for the hopes,
  the efforts and the achievements
  which your Spirit of peace
  has inspired in our days
  – stirring up love where there was hatred,

sympathy where there was suspicion,
care where there was indifference.

2 Open our minds and our hearts even more
   to the specific demands
   which love for others makes upon us,
   so that we may be more truly
   makers of peace.

3 Remember, God of mercies,
   those who are oppressed,
   those who are suffering and dying
   for the birth of a world
   in which all people
   will be more truly
   a single human family.

4 May your kingdom come
   for all people of every race and language
   – your kingdom of justice, of peace, of love,
   and may all the earth be filled with your glory.
   We make our prayer through Jesus Christ,
   the Prince of Peace. Amen.

Blessing   NH   **185**

Father of all mankind,
   you look with great love on all your people
   of whatever race, culture and religion.
We ask you to bless us this day
   and send your Holy Spirit upon us
   and upon all the diverse peoples of our world:
   the Spirit of peace and justice,
   of understanding and reconciliation.
May people of violence
   allow themselves to be touched
   by the plight of those who suffer,
   and may your Spirit help broaden the horizons
   and deepen the understanding of us all.
We make this our prayer
   through Jesus, the Prince of Peace. Amen.

The prayer, *'Father, you have made all people in your own likeness'* (181), refers to Gen 1^{27}, Wis 2^{23}; Wis 11^{24}; Lk 2; Mt 2^{1-12}; Lk 7^{10}, Mk 7^{26}; Lk 17^{19}, Lk 10^{36}; Jn 12^{20}; Lk 23^{26}; Jn 11^{52}; Gen 1^{27}, Wis 2^{23}; Lk 1^{48}, Jn 15^{15}; Lk 24^{31}; 1 Pet 3^8, 1 Jn 4^{20}

The blessing, *'Father of all mankind'* (185), was written in response to the events of 11th September 2001.

Gathering in the Presence of God

NH
cf Mt 18[19]

May the Lord, whose presence has been keenly felt by Christians down the ages, help us to appreciate that he is, indeed, with us now as *'two or three gather in his name'* to pray.

(pause)

Prayer

NH   **186**

1   God our Father,
    if I could trace back
    through the last two thousand years,
    marking out routes from Jesus himself
    and then through people
    whose faith has touched others
    and so reached me,
    I would be astounded
    by the individuals I would encounter.

2   I give thanks, Father,
    for all those people
    over two thousand years
    who have inspired others
    and played their part
    in passing on to generation after generation
    the living heritage of their faith.

3   Especially I give thanks
    for those who have lived their faith
    through difficulties and hardship and persecution.

4   I pray, Father, that I may grow
    in your faith and love
    through good times and bad. Amen.

Prayer

Bishop Timothy   **187**
Dudley-Smith

1   For all links in the chain, O Lord my God,
        that brought to me
        the story of the gospel
        – **I thank you, Father, with all my heart.**

2 For Christ himself,
   author and finisher of our faith;
   for Christ who is himself
   the good news for all mankind
   – I thank you, Father, with all my heart.

3 For saints and martyrs, teachers and evangelists;
   for that apostolic company;
   and for Paul, "unfit to be called an apostle"
   – I thank you, Father, with all my heart.

4 And so it goes on, and always at a price.
   In toil and labour, in pain and blood,
      the good news spreads from place to place,
      generation to generation.
   For all who shared in the missionary task
      – I thank you, Father, with all my heart.

5 And for my chance to be – myself –
   a link in this great chain,
   a bearer of good news of Christ to others
      – I thank you, Father, with all my heart.
      And may it be a heart of love,
      of joy, of praise! Amen.

188 Silent Reflection

Pope John Paul II

We need heralds of the Gospel
who are experts in humanity,
who know the depths of the human heart,
who can share
the joys, the hopes, the agonies, the distress
of people today,
but who are, at the same time, contemplative
and have fallen in love with God.

189 Prayer

Pope Paul VI

1 Let us preserve our fervour of spirit.
  Let us preserve
  the delightful and comforting joy of evangelising,
  even when it is in tears that we must sow.

2 May it mean for us
  – as it did for John the Baptist, for Peter and Paul,
  for the other apostles,

and for a multitude of splendid evangelisers
all through the Church's history –
an interior enthusiasm
that nobody and nothing can quench.

3   May it be the great joy of our consecrated lives.
    And may the world of our time, which is searching
    – sometimes with anguish, sometimes with hope –
    be enabled to receive the Good News,

4   not from evangelisers who are dejected,
    discouraged, impatient or anxious,
    but from ministers of the Gospel
    whose lives glow with fervour,
    who have first received the joy of Christ,

5   and who are willing to risk their lives
    so that the Kingdom may be proclaimed,
    and the Church established in the midst of the world.

ALL   ***Glory be to the Father, and to the Son,***
        and to the Holy Spirit,
        as it was in the beginning, is now, and ever shall be,
        world without end. Amen.

Prayer

Reflection on Psalm 111 **190**
Kevin Lyon

1   I do not pray alone, Lord;
        I pray with my brothers and sisters
        who work together
        for the coming of your Kingdom.

2   I make mine the prayers of each,
        while they make my prayers their own,
        giving prayer a new meaning:
        a new dimension, a new depth.

3   Even getting together in your presence, Lord,
        is itself a prayer.
    When we pray, the whole world prays.
    We know its needs; we live its aspirations.
    All who suffer the same evils
        need the same blessings.
    There is no selfishness in common prayer.

4   Bless us, Lord, and bless the efforts we make
        for the coming of your Kingdom.

191 Blessing

cf 2 Thess 3^{16,18}

May the Lord himself
    give us peace at all times
    and in every way.
May the grace of our Lord, Jesus Christ,
    be with us all. Amen.

The Kingdom grows amongst us

Gathering in the Presence of God

NH 192

> The apostles were called to keep close company with Jesus
> and he had a special affection for them.
> Called to serve as apostles,
> we are invited to be with Jesus
> and grow in friendship with him.
> Let us remind ourselves that he is with us now,

ALL   **and let us adore him.**

(pause)

Prayer

Ephesians 4[1-7,11-13] 193
(J B Phillips)

1 I beg you to live lives worthy of your high calling.
   Accept life with humility and patience,
     making allowances for each other
     because you love one another.

2 Make it your aim to be at one in the Spirit,
     and you will inevitably be at peace with one another.
   You all belong to one Body, of which there is one Spirit,
     just as you all experienced one calling to one hope.

3 There is one Lord, one faith, one baptism,
     one God, one Father of us all,
     who is the One over all,
     the One working through all,
     and the One living in all.

4 Naturally there are different gifts and functions.
   Individually grace is given to us in different ways
     out of the rich diversity of Christ's giving.

5 His gifts were varied.
   Some he made special messengers, some prophets,
     some preachers of the Gospel;
     to some he gave the power to guide and teach his people.

6 His gifts were made
     that Christians might be properly equipped for their service,
     that the whole Body might be built up,
     until the time comes when, in the unity of common faith

and common knowledge of the Son of God,
we arrive at real maturity
– that measure of development
which is meant by 'the fullness of Christ'.

Glory be…

194 Prayer

1 We praise you, Father, for those
who are poor in spirit; who seek to discover what you want of them;
who give to others more than they receive;
who are humble and whose intentions are pure;
who promote justice, peace, and reconciliation,
and bring joy to the lives of those around them.

We praise you, Father, as we see your kingdom grow among us.

2 We rejoice, Father, in those who listen gladly,
and who look with understanding and love;
in those who look beyond the superficial,
who seek and find the positive and the good in all people –
for they act justly, love tenderly, and walk humbly with you, Father.

We praise you, Father, as we see your kingdom grow among us.

3 We thank you, Father,
for those who are grafted to Jesus your Son,
and bear good fruit that endures:
those for whom the serving and loving of others
has become a natural and instinctive part of their lives –
those who touch hearts and build up and renew;
who welcome people and restore dignity;
who encourage the weak and lighten burdens.

We praise you, Father, as we see your kingdom grow among us.

4 We thank you, Father, for those who shine like the sun:
those who see and value others
as being made in your image and likeness;
those who accept others without conditions and without judgment;
those who respect the vulnerable and the marginalised;
and for those who forgive other people from the heart
with the love that you bring in your forgiveness, Father.

We praise you, Father, as we see your kingdom grow among us.

5   We praise you for those who develop their talents and abilities;
        for those who appreciate themselves and look for your kingdom within,
            who treasure what is of lasting value;
        who pray at home and in the solitude of their hearts,
            seeking a living relationship with you, Father –
            no longer believing simply because of what others have told them;
        who are willing to change and start afresh:
            for those who pray and live in such a way
            that your kingdom comes to fruition in their lives.

We praise you, Father, as we see your kingdom grow among us.

6   We are grateful for those in our midst who are like little children
            in their qualities of trust and dependence on you, Father,
            and who live in such a way
            that shows that your love surrounds them.
        We praise you, Father, for those whose wealth is your love;
        for those who know that nothing can separate them from your love,
            who live in your friendship and in your presence;
        for those in whose frailty we see your strength,
            who remain faithful and patient,
            delighting in all things,
            living prayerfully and being thankful.

We praise you, Father, as we see your kingdom grow among us.

7   We thank you, Father, for those who influence us for good,
            proclaiming your Kingdom in the silent witness of their lives,
            who give themselves in joyful sacrifice,
            loving others and not counting the cost,
            treating others as they themselves would like to be treated,
            loving and praying for those who may not return that love
            – for they know that love never gives up.
        We thank you for those who bring healing to those entrusted to them
            and for those who see young people as a gift and a real blessing.

We praise you, Father, as we see your kingdom grow among us.

195 Blessing A Celtic Blessing

May the encircling Father be with us
  – the encircling power of the Creator.
May the enfolding Christ be round us
  – the enfolding arms of his love.
May the enabling Spirit be round us
  – the enabling of the strength of God. Amen.

Paragraphs of Prayer 194

(1) Mt 5, Lk 2^{10}

(2) Mk 12^{37}, Mt 13^{13}, Mk 10^{21}, Lk 5^{26}, Lk 19^{1-10},21^{1-4}; Mic 6^8

(3) Jn 15^{16}, Mt 25^{34-40}

(4) Mt 13^{43}; Gen 1^{27}; Mt 7^1; Lk 18^{15},19^5; Mt 18^{32-33}, Lk 11^4

(5) Mt 25^{14-30}; Lk 17^{21}; Mt 13^{45}, 6^{20}; Mt 6^6, Lk 5^{16}; Jn 4^{42}; Mk 1^4, Jn 3^3; Mt 6^{10}

(6) Mk 10^{15}; Mk 10^{17-31}; Rom 8^{39}; Jn 15^5, Jms 2^{23}, Ps 139, Jn 17^{26}; Jn 20^{30};
     2 Cor 4^7; Lk 16^{10}; 1 Thess 5^{16-18}

(7) Mt 5^{13-16}; Lk 9^{60}; Lk 6^{20-26}; Jn 11^{35}; Mt 7^{12}; Mt 5^{44}; 1 Cor 13^7; Mt 4^{23};
     Ps 127^3

104   WALK IN MY PRESENCE

Gathering in the Presence of God

NH
cf Mk 2[1-12]

196

Like the paralysed man, Lord,
>friends lower us from the roof
>so that we can be right in front of you.
Your love and understanding,
>your gaze and your smile
>bring us your healing,
>and we rejoice to be with you now.

(pause)

Prayer

Michael Buckley

197

Jesus, your coming on earth
>was like a new dawn over a world of darkness;
>the blind saw,
>the lame walked again,
>the sick were healed,
>and even the dead were raised to life.
Come again into the lives of everyone
>and heal the wounds of our broken hearts.
Come again to all who are sick or depressed,
>and fill their lives with hope and peace.
Come again to us
>as we call on your holy name,
>so that we, too,
>may receive your help and healing grace. Amen.

Prayer

NH

198

1 God our Father,
>we bring before you today
>those who suffer from chronic illness or disability
>– those for whom sickness or disability
>profoundly affects their lives.
>When they feel diminished,
>>**remind them that you call them by name**
>>**and hold them**
>>**in the palm of your hand.**

Is 43[1]

2   When they feel fragile and broken,
    mould them and heal them,
    that they may more closely resemble
    the image of Jesus,
    your Son and our Brother.

3   When they are reminded
    of different times in the past,
    lead them to grow in the faith
    that you love them today, as they are,
    in the reality of their lives this day.

4   When they feel uncertain about the future,
    lead them to that perfect love   1 John 4[18]
    which casts out all fear.

5   When situations remind them
    – not of what they *can* do,
    but of what they *cannot* do –
    remind them that "love never fails",   1 Cor 13[8]
    and that, living in your love,
    they will bear your fruit in plenty.

6   May all of us, Father,
    – whatever our circumstances –
    never be so taken up with our own concerns
    that we do not see
    or respond to the needs of others.
    May we live with courage   Jn 15[5,9]
    the various challenges
    that we face each day. Amen.

199 Reading

Pope John Paul II

Today I make an urgent plea to this nation.
Do not neglect your sick and elderly.
Do not turn away from the handicapped and dying.
Do not push them to the margins of society.
For, if you do, you will fail to understand
    that they represent an important truth.
The sick, the elderly, the handicapped and the dying
    teach us that weakness is a creative part of human living,
    and that suffering can be embraced with no loss of dignity.
Without the presence of these people in your midst,
    you might be tempted to think of health, strength and power

as the only important values to be pursued in life.
But the wisdom of Christ and the power of Christ
are to be seen in the weakness of those who share his sufferings.

Prayer

Cardinal Basil Hume, OSB **200**

1   Lord God, almighty Creator,
    teach me and all people
    to understand more and more profoundly
    that every human life is sacred,
    whether it belongs to an unborn infant
    or to a terminally-ill patient,
    to a handicapped child
    or to a disabled adult.

2   Remind us, heavenly Father,
    that each individual
    has been made in your image and likeness
    and has been redeemed by Christ.

3   Help us to see each other with your eyes
    so that we may reverence, preserve and sustain
    your gift of life in them
    and use our own lives more faithfully in your service. Amen.

Intercessions

NH **201**

1   We pray, Lord, that your work of healing may continue
        through the hands of those who minister to the sick and aged.
    Above all, give them the desire
        to understand those who are not well.
    Lord, in your mercy – *hear our prayer*.

2   Look in kindness, Father,
        on those who suffer from constant sickness or weakness
        and on those who see no progress and never get well.
    Give them courage and generosity
        and lead them to remain positive
        in carrying their cross for the salvation of the world.
    Lord, in your mercy – *hear our prayer*.

3   We pray for ourselves,
        that we may live in cheerfulness and patience
        in times of good health and bad.
    Bring your healing touch, Lord,
        to those we know to be sick, afraid or worried.
    Lord, in your mercy – *hear our prayer*.

202 Blessing

2 Cor 13[13]

May the grace of our Lord Jesus Christ
and the love of the Father
and the fellowship of the Holy Spirit
be with us all. Amen.

The busy day takes its rest
– an evening/night prayer

Gathering in the Presence of God

Aware of the beauty of our earth and of what the night sky can reveal, we remind ourselves that the Creator of the stars of the universe invites us to call him *'Father'*. Let us remind ourselves in the silence of our hearts that he is with us…

(pause)

Prayer

May none of God's wonderful works keep silence,
    night or morning.
Bright stars, high mountains,
    the depths of the seas, sources of rushing rivers:
    may all these break into song
    as we sing to Father, Son and Holy Spirit.
May the angels in heaven reply: 'Amen!'
All power, praise, honour and eternal glory
    be to God, the only Giver of grace. Amen.

Personal Reflection

1 In 'Jane Eyre', Charlotte Bronte wrote: *"We know that God is everywhere, but certainly we feel his presence most when his works are on the grandest scale spread before us, and it is in the unclouded night-sky, where his worlds wheel their silent course, that we read clearest his infinitude, his omnipotence, his omnipresence."*

2 St Ignatius Loyola could not look at the stars in the night sky without being moved to tears by God's beauty.

Reading

1 I shall never forget the nights under the Saharan stars. I felt as if I were wrapped around by the blanket of the friendly night, a blanket embroidered with stars. Yes, a friendly night, a benevolent darkness with restful shadows. In them the movement of my soul is not hindered. On the contrary, it can spread out, be fulfilled, grow and be joyful. I feel at home, safe, fearless, desirous only of staying like this for hours; my only worry that of the shortness of the night, so avid am I to read within and outside myself the symbols of divine language.

2 The friendly night is an image of faith, that gift of God defined: *'The guarantee*

of the blessings we hope for and proof of the existence of the realities that at present remain unseen' (Hebrews 11:1). I have never found a better metaphor for my relationship with the eternal: a point lost in infinite space, wrapped round by the night under the subdued light of the stars. I am this point lost in space: the darkness, like an irreplaceable friend, is faith; the stars, God's witness.

3   When my faith was weak, all this would have seemed incomprehensible to me. I was afraid as a child is of the night. But now I have conquered it, and it is mine. I experience joy in night, navigating upon it as upon the sea. The night is no longer my enemy, nor does it make me afraid. On the contrary, its darkness and divine transcendence are a source of delight.

4   Sometimes I even close my eyes to see more darkness. I know the stars are there in their place, as a witness to me of heaven. And I can see why darkness is so necessary. The darkness is necessary, the darkness of faith is necessary, for God's light is too great. It wounds. I understand more and more that faith is not a mysterious and cruel trick of a God who hides himself without telling me why, but a necessary veil. My discovery of him takes place gradually, respecting the growth of divine life in me.

207 **Prayer**
Bruce Prewer

1   The busy day now takes its rest,
        as mother-evening enfolds us in embrace.
    The distant stars and galaxies
        signal messages about a Creator so vast
        that our minds stagger
        and our hearts are filled with loving awe.

2   O Lord, our Lord,
        glorious is your name in all the universe.   cf Ps 8

3   What are earth's children
        that you notice us?
    And what is the mystery of divine grace
        that you love us?

4   You give us faith to trust you,
        even though we cannot see you.
    You touch our minds with fingers of light,
        and our hearts with forgiveness and peace.

5   As the evening moves on, we go to rest,
        able to sleep the sleep of children

who know that, in life or death,
we are surrounded by love eternal.

6   O Lord, our Lord, glorious is your name
on earth and in the heavens!

Prayer

Bernard Thorogood   208

Dear God, you are always surprising me.
My day was just a few hours of life,
    yet in it you were teaching me new things.
You showed me a fresh aspect of familiar people I met,
    and new truth about myself.
Forgive my slowness to understand your word;
    don't add up the wasted minutes;
    judge all my work with a father's mercy.
Thank you, Lord, for the light and the night;
    enable me to find renewal in sleep,
    and let me know, deep in my heart,
    that tomorrow I will be with you. Amen.

Prayer

Leslie F Brandt   209

1   The day is over, O God,
        and I commit its failures
        as well as its successes
        into your hands.

2   I rejoice in your tender care
        and celebrate your loving presence.
    I pray that you will heal the wounds
        of those I have hurt,
        and enrich the lives of those I have helped.

3   I place in your care those I love most
        and those through whom
        you ministered to me this day.
    Bless them and keep them and fill their lives with joy.

4   I pray that you may somehow reach those
        whom I couldn't love or cause to feel my love,
        that other faithful servants of yours
        may convey your concern for them.

5   Grant that I may truly learn how to love
        as you love me,

and demonstrate that love
to the lonely, despairing people in my path.

ALL *This day is over, O God,*
its blessings and conflicts and disappointments.
If it is within your will, grant me another,
and help me to live it in your strength
and according to your plan,
through Jesus Christ our Lord. Amen.

210 Blessing

May the Lord of creation bless us this night.
May he restore us in our sleep
that tomorrow we may share the word of life
and shine like stars   Phil 2$^{15\text{-}16}$
in the world that he loves so much. Amen.   Jn 3^{16}

Even at night you direct my heart

Ps 16[7]

Gathering in the Presence of God

NH   211

Lord, it is not that we are somehow
    placing ourselves in your presence.
Instead we are asking
    that you help us become more aware
    that you are already with us.

(pause)

Prayer

Lucien Deiss   212

Lord Jesus,
    I would have chosen, like Mary,
    to sit all day long in peace at your feet,
    and listen to the silence of my heart.

But you came into my house
    with all your friends
    who kept me busy,
    and I served them for love of you.

If I cannot offer you the eyes of Mary,
    accept at least, I pray you,
    the tired hands of Martha.
They are my love for you.

Personal Reflection – *on Psalm 63*

John Brook   213

With intense longing the psalmist expresses his desire for the presence of God…
The psalmist is as thirsty for God as the land is for water in a parched desert…

"So I gaze on you in the sanctuary, to see your strength and your glory."
    The references may be to a unique experience of God's glory, such as that
    described in Isaiah 6[1-10], when the prophet *"saw the Lord seated on a high
    and lofty throne; his train filled the sanctuary… and the Temple was full of
    smoke."* Or it may refer to a more common experience, where the psalmist
    sees God's strength and glory symbolised in the Ark of the Covenant, or in
    the Temple liturgy with its splendid music, drama and sacrifice. The
    Christian coming to the Eucharist thinks instinctively of the presence of
    Christ in the consecrated bread, lifted up by the priest… We gaze on him
    in the sanctuary to see his strength and glory.

"In your name I will lift up my hands."

The lifting up of both hands was the traditional posture of prayer, and a visible sign of the psalmist's longing that his empty hands would be filled with God's blessings...

"On my bed I remember you. On you I muse through the night."

The night hours have traditionally been a time of testing, a time when human defences are low, and when the pull to evil seems stronger. So the psalmist deliberately decides to meditate in the night on the Lord, to turn to him for help...

"In the shadow of your wings I rejoice."

The *"wings"* may be the wings of a mother bird protecting her chicks, or the wings of the gold cherubim above the Ark of the Covenant in the sanctuary of the Temple. The psalmist rejoices in the protection of the presence of the Lord.

214 Psalm 63$^{1-9}$

Antiphon: Even at night you will direct my heart.

1 O God, you are my God, for you I long;
   for you my soul is thirsting.
   My body pines for you
   like a dry, weary land without water.
   So I gaze on you in the sanctuary
   to see your strength and your glory.

2 For your love is better than life,
   my lips will speak your praise.
   So I will bless you all my life,
   in your name I will lift up my hands.
   My soul shall be filled as with a banquet,
   my mouth shall praise you with joy.

3 On my bed I remember you.
   On you I muse through the night
   for you have been my help;
   in the shadow of your wings I rejoice.
   My soul clings to you;
   your right hand holds me fast.

   Glory be...

Antiphon: Even at night you will direct my heart.

Ps 16^{7}

Intercessions

1 Lord, we ask you to bless those who will have little or no sleep tonight.
We pray for medics who are called out on duty
and for all the emergency services who protect us from danger
on land, on water, and in the air.
Lord, in your mercy – **hear our prayer**.

2 We pray for those who work through the night for our convenience:
all who are caring for those in hospital,
those who work in the energy and utility services,
those who are distributing fresh food across the country,
postal workers and all in the communications media.
Lord, in your mercy – **hear our prayer**.

3 We pray for individuals who will sleep in the open tonight,
and who have no comfort.
Lord, in your mercy – **hear our prayer**.

4 We pray for those who will be able to sleep little tonight
because of worry, pain or illness.
Lord, in your mercy – **hear our prayer**.

Prayer   Donal Neary, SJ   216

1 This evening, Lord, I give you thanks:
for the good things of today,
for people whose friendship I value,
for the work well done, for deadlines met,
for home and for shelter, for the food I ate.

2 May the darkness of tonight
take with it the bitterness of today.
May sunset put to rest my anger,
and the starlight be a reminder
that your forgiveness never fails.
For my failure in your service this day,
I ask your forgiveness.

3 I see now that you were present to me this day –
in the love of those I met,
in the call to sympathise and console,
in the cries of those poorer than I:
those who have no friends, no food, no home, no shelter.
I remember them now, Lord, in your presence.

ALL *For today, Lord, thanks – and sorry.*
I put to rest with you the troubles of this day.
I ask for the peace of your presence
until the new day dawns.
May the protection you give at the end of a day
be with me and my loved ones
all the days of our lives. Amen.

217 Blessing

NH

May the Lord Jesus
– who told us not to be anxious or afraid
but to seek first his kingdom
and lay our burdens on him –
now bless us and give us rest.
May he transform any pain or sorrow
and bring us healing in our sleep. Amen.

Watch our sleeping, guard our waking

– a night prayer

Gathering in the Presence of God

David Adam   218

1 In you we live and move;
     in you we have our being.
  We are in your love,
     enfolded in your peace,
     surrounded by your might.

2 Open our eyes, Lord;
     enlarge our vision.
  Open our hearts, Lord;
     increase our faith.
  Open our minds, Lord;
     deepen our knowing.

3 We are in your love,
     enfolded in your peace,
     surrounded by your might.
  In you we live and move;
     in you we have our being.

Acts 17[28]

(pause)

Prayer

Lucien Deiss   219

1 We thank you, Lord, for this day
     filled with your presence.

2 We praise and bless you
     for the joy of those who love one another,
     for the efforts of those who work,
     for the patience of those who suffer,
     for every good work
       that people have accomplished in your honour today.

3 We ask pardon of you
     for the weakness of our love
     on the road that leads to you.

4   Lead us beyond the night
        to the dawn of eternal day
        when we will see you face to face.

220 Personal Reflection

Cardinal Lustiger

Just before falling off to sleep, form with your lips and store in your heart a verse of the Psalm that you have chosen for nourishment, and wake up with it. While you sleep, this presence of the Word of God will search out in the depths of your consciousness all that you have not succeeded in bringing up to the light of day, and it will be illuminated with the light of God the Saviour. As you rest, those words will produce fruit, much more than you could ever imagine. Just as Isaiah prophesied:

> *"So shall my word be that goes forth from my mouth;*
> *it shall not return to me empty,*
> *but it shall accomplish that for which I purpose it,*
> *and prosper in the thing for which I sent it."*

And Jesus says to us:

> *"The Kingdom of God*
> *is as if a man should scatter seed upon the ground,*
> *and should sleep and rise night and day,*
> *and the seed should sprout and grow, he knows not how."*

221 Psalm 147ᴮ

Antiphon: My word shall not return to me empty
                but shall accomplish that for which I sent it.

Is 55[11]

O praise the Lord, Jerusalem,
Zion, praise your God!

He has strengthened the bars of your gates,
he has blessed the children within you.
He established peace on your borders,
he feeds you with finest wheat.

He sends out his word to the earth
and swiftly runs his command.
He showers down snow white as wool,
he scatters hoarfrost like ashes.

He hurls down hailstones like crumbs.
The waters are frozen at his touch;
he sends forth his word and it melts them:
at the breath of his mouth the waters flow.

He makes his word known to Jacob,
to Israel his laws and decrees.
He has not dealt thus with other nations;
he has not taught them his decrees.

Glory be…

Antiphon: My word shall not return to me empty
but shall accomplish that for which I sent it.

Prayer

NH   **222**
based on a prayer by
St Gregory Nazianzen

Whilst I am asleep, Lord,
   I want my heart still to turn to you.
Be present throughout my sleep,
   permeating all the recesses of my mind.
Use my time of sleep
   to work on all that is deep within me.
By your healing touch
   re-create and restore me this night.
Bring me closer to you and make me whole.
Then I will awake
   and be able to join the angels and all of creation
   in proclaiming your greatness.

Personal Reflection

223

*I might wish to choose a phrase (such as one of the following) as a simple prayer
to repeat slowly as I fall asleep:*

1   Into your hands, Lord,
     I commend my spirit.

Ps 31[6]

2   Lord, you heal the broken-hearted
     and bind up all our wounds.

Ps 147[3]

Blessing

NH   **224**

1   Father, you heal the broken-hearted
      and bind up all our wounds.
   Bless us this night
      and touch us deep within
      whilst we sleep.

2   Burn away our pretence
      and restore our vision.
   Soothe our hurts

and calm our fears.
Heal our memories
and make us whole.

3   Mould us and re-create us
so that we grow closer in likeness
to Jesus, your Son,
in whose radiant face
you can see all of mankind.

ALL   Bless us, Father, this night
as we lay all our concerns in your hands.
Empower us with your Spirit in the day ahead,
that we may convey your love and healing
to those whose lives we will share. Amen.

Other 'arrow' prayers that might be used (223) could include the following:

3   I thank you, Lord,
for your faithfulness and love. *(Ps 103^8)*

4   Lord, you are close to the broken-hearted;
those whose spirit is crushed you will save. *(Ps 34^{18})*

5   Jesus, remember me
when you come into your kingdom. *(Lk 23^{42})*

6   Lord, you know that I love you. *(Jn 21^{15})*

Hymns

A1

Be still and know
Colours of day
I watch the sunrise
Lord, as I awake
Lord, for tomorrow and its needs
Lord of all hopefulness
May you walk with Christ beside you
Morning is broken
New daytime dawning
O come, let us follow
Take my life and let it be
The light of Christ
This day God gives me
This is the day

A2

Be still and know
Colours of day
I give my hands
In him we knew a fullness
Lord, as I awake
Lord, for tomorrow and its needs
Lord of all hopefulness
May you walk with Christ beside you
Morning is broken
O come, let us follow
Take my hands
Take my life and let it be
This day God gives me
This is the day

A3

Alone with only you, my God
Be not afraid
Be still and know I am with you
Brother, sister, let me serve you
Christ be beside me
Christ be near at either hand
Deep within

Do not be afraid
Father, in my life I see
Give us, Lord, a new heart
He who would valiant be
I bind unto myself today
In your coming and going
I will be with you
I will come to you in the silence
Jesus, you are Lord
Lead, kindly light
Lord of all hopefulness
Lord of creation, to you be all praise
May you walk with Christ beside you
Moses, I know you're the man
My Lord, my Master
O come let us follow
Oh the Word of my Lord
On the journey to Emmaus
Walk with me, O my Lord
We walk by faith
Yahweh, I know you are near
You are near

A4

Alone with only you, my God
Be not afraid
Be still and know I am with you
Brother, sister, let me serve you
Christ be beside me
Christ be near at either hand
Colours of day
Guide me, O thou great Redeemer
Did not our hearts
Do not be afraid
Father, in my life I see
He who would valiant be
I bind unto myself today
In your coming and going
I will be with you
I will come to you in the silence

Jesus, you are Lord
Lead, kindly light
Lord of all hopefulness
Lord of creation, to you be all praise
May you walk with Christ beside you
Moses, I know you're the man
My Lord, my Master
O come let us follow
Oh the Word of my Lord
On the journey to Emmaus
Sing it in the valleys
Sing of one who walks beside us
Walk with me, O my Lord
We walk by faith
Yahweh, I know you are near
You are near

A5

A new commandment
Brother, sister, let me serve you
Forth in thy name
If I am lacking love
Lord, make me a means
Love is his word
Make me a channel
Praise to the Lord, the almighty
This is my will, my one command
Whatsoever you do
Will you come and follow me

A6

Be still and know
Be still for the presence of the Lord
Blest be the Lord
Dear Lord and Father of mankind
In you, my God
I will be with you
Lord Jesus Christ, your light
My soul is longing for your peace
O Lord, you search me
On eagle's wings
Yahweh, I know you are near
You know me, Lord

A7

Amazing grace
Be not afraid
Blest be the Lord
Come down, O love divine
Do not be afraid
For to those who love God
If God is for us
In you, my God
I will come to you in the silence
I will never forget you
Oh the love of my Lord
On eagle's wings
Only a shadow
Sing of the Lord's goodness
The light of Christ
There's a kindness in God's mercy
Yahweh, I know you are near
Yahweh's love will last forever

A8

Because the Lord is my shepherd
(Gelineau Psalm 23)
Glory to God who does wondrous things
Like a shepherd
Now the day has drawn to ending
O Christe, Domine Jesu (Taizé)
Shepherd me, O God
The king of love
The Lord's my shepherd

A9

Abba, abba Father, you are the potter
Blest be the Lord
Earthen vessels
Father, I place into your hands
Father, I put my life in your hands
Glory to God who does wondrous things
I give my hands
On eagle's wings
Take my hands
Take my life and let it be

A10

Brother, sister, let me serve you
Come, come, follow me
Follow me, follow me
God's Spirit is in my heart
Happy are those who are invited
Here I am, Lord
My God said to me, 'Follow'
My soul is longing for your peace
Only a shadow
The kingdom of heaven
Will you come and follow me

A11

Be thou my vision
Blest be the Lord
Come, come, follow me
Come down, O love divine
Come to me, O weary traveller
Come to set us free
Follow me
If God is for us
Lord God, you love us
My soul is longing for your peace
This, then, is my prayer
We walk by faith

A12

Amazing grace
Be thou my vision
Christ is our king, let the whole world
Come down, O love divine
God of mercy and compassion
God, whose almighty Word
I saw the grass
I watch the sunrise
Lord of creation, to you be all praise
We walk by faith
Yahweh is the God of my salvation

A13

Be still for the presence of the Lord
Did not our hearts
Earthen vessels

How good, Lord, to be here
I have loved you
Into one we all are gathered
On eagle's wings
Shine, Jesus, shine
Those who seek your face
We behold the splendour of God

A14

All creatures of our God and king
All the earth proclaims the Lord
Colours of day
Come, come, follow me
I watch the sunrise
I will sing a song
Let us sing to the Lord *(Taizé)*
Oh Lord my God, the Father
O worship the king
Shine, Jesus, shine
Sing a new song unto the Lord
The heavens are telling
We cannot own the sunlit sky

A15

All the earth proclaim the Lord
God beyond all names
I sing the almighty power of God
I watch the sunrise
I will sing a song
Let us sing to the Lord *(Taizé)*
Oh Lord my God, the Father
O Lord my God, when I in awesome
O worship the king
Sing to the mountains
Surrexit Christus *(Taizé)*
The heavens are telling
To God with gladness sing
We cannot own the sunlit sky
We plough the fields and scatter

A16

All the earth proclaim the Lord
God beyond all names
I sing the almighty power of God

I watch the sunrise
I will sing a song
Let us sing to the Lord *(Taizé)*
Oh Lord my God, the Father
O Lord my God, when I in awesome
O worship the king
Sing to the mountains
Surrexit Christus *(Taizé)*
The heavens are telling
To God with gladness sing
We cannot own the sunlit sky
We plough the fields and scatter

A17

All creatures of our God and King
All the earth proclaim the Lord
Father, I place into your hands
God beyond all names
I give my hands
I sing the almighty power of God
I watch the sunrise
I will sing a song
Let us sing to the Lord *(Taizé)*
Oh Lord my God, the Father
O Lord my God, when I in awesome
O worship the king
Sing to the mountains
Surrexit Christus *(Taizé)*
Thanks be to God
The heavens are telling
To God with gladness sing
We cannot own the sunlit sky
We plough the fields and scatter

A18

Be not afraid
Darkness falls, my hour has come
Deep within
Do not be afraid
Give me a new heart
Give us, Lord, a new heart
God's Spirit is in my heart
Grant to us, O Lord, a heart
Here I am, Lord

Now the green blade
O God beyond all praising
On the journey to Emmaus
Seek ye first
Spirit of God within me
This, then, is my prayer
Yahweh, I know you are near
You are near

A19

All that I counted as gain
A new commandment
Darkness falls, my hour has come
If God is for us
If I am lacking love
Now the green blade
This is my will, my one command
Ubi caritas *(Taizé)*
Where there is love, there is God
Will you come and follow me

A20

A new commandment
Brother, sister, let me serve you
If I am lacking love
Now it is evening
O Lord, all the world belongs
This is what Yahweh asks
The Lord hears the cry of the poor
Whatsoever you do
When I needed a neighbour

A21

A new commandment
Brother, sister, let me serve you
Go tell everyone
If I am lacking love
Lord, make me a means
Make me a channel
Now it is evening
O Lord, all the world belongs
Peace, perfect peace
The Lord hears the cry of the poor
This is what Yahweh asks

Whatsoever you do
When I needed a neighbour

A22

A new commandment
Christ's is the world in which we move
For the healing of the nations
If I am lacking love
Look around you, can you see?
Lord Jesus Christ, upon the night
Now watch for God's coming
O comfort my people
O Lord, all the world belongs
Tell out my soul
The Lord hears the cry of the poor
The voice of God goes out
This is what Yahweh asks
Whatsoever you do

A23

A new commandment
Christ's is the world in which we move
For the healing of the nations
If I am lacking love
Look around you, can you see?
Lord, make me a means
Make me a channel
O Lord, all the world belongs
Praise to the Father the source of all life
Tell out my soul
The Lord hears the cry of the poor
The voice of God goes out
This is what Yahweh asks
Whatsoever you do

A24

All you nations, sing out your joy
A new commandment
Be still and know I am with you
Christ's is the world in which we move
Come, let us go up to the Lord
Diverse in culture
For the healing of the nations
Into one we all are gathered

I will sing a song
Laudate Dominum *(Taizé)*
Look around you, can you see?
Lord, for the years
Lord, make me a means
Make me a channel
Now watch for God's coming
O comfort my people
Sing of the Lord's goodness
The Lord hears the cry of the poor
The voice of God goes out
This is my will, my one command

A25

Adoramus Te, Domine *(Taizé)*
Alleluia, give thanks to the risen Lord
Blessed are they
Bring forth the kingdom
Celtic Alleluia *(Te Deum)*
Christ is our king, let the whole world
City of God
Come, come, follow me
Follow me
Forth in the peace of Christ
For you are my God
Gather us in *(not v.3)*
God and man at table are sat down
God has chosen me
God's Spirit is in my heart
Great is the power we proclaim
Here I am, Lord
Into one we all are gathered
I will sing a song
Lord, for the years
My God said to me, 'Follow'
Oh the Word of my Lord
O Lord, all the world
One bread, one body
Out of darkness
Rejoice, rejoice, Christ is in you
Seek ye first
The kingdom of God
The Servant King
This is my will, my one command

Thy hand, O God, has guided
We are God's work of art
We come to you, Lord
We praise you, O God (Te Deum)
Yahweh's love will last forever
You are called to tell the story

A26

Alleluia, give thanks to the risen Lord
Blessed are they
Bring forth the kingdom
Christ is our king, let the whole world
City of God
Come, come, follow me
Follow me
Forth in the peace of Christ
Gather us in (not v.3)
God has chosen me
God's Spirit is in my heart
Great is the power we proclaim
Here I am, Lord
Into one we all are gathered
I will sing a song
Laudate omnes gentes (Taizé)
Lord, for the years
My God said to me, 'Follow'
Oh the Word of my Lord
O Lord, all the world
One bread, one body
Our God sent his Son long ago
Out of darkness
Rejoice, rejoice, Christ is in you
Seek ye first
Tell out my soul
The kingdom of God
The kingdom of heaven
The Servant King
This is my will, my one command
We are God's work of art
We come to you, Lord
Will you come and follow me
You are called to tell the story

A27

Be still and know
By gracious powers
Come to me, O weary traveller
For to those who love God
Healer of our every ill
If God is for us
I will sing a song
Lay your hands
Oh the Word of my Lord
O let all who thirst
Though the mountains may fall
Your hands, O Lord, in days of old

A28

As the setting sun
Day is done
Dear Lord and Father of mankind
Father, I place into your hands
In your coming and going
I watch the sunrise
I will sing a song
Lord of all hopefulness
Now it is evening
Now the day has drawn to ending
Oh Lord my God, the Father of creation
Oh the love of my Lord
O Lord my God, when I in awesome
Round me falls the night
The day thou gavest
You who sleep, rise up, alleluia

A29

As the setting sun
Day is done
Dear Lord and Father of mankind
Do not worry over what to eat
In your coming and going
I watch the sunrise
Lord of all hopefulness
Now it is evening
Now the day has drawn to ending
Oh the love of my Lord
Round me falls the night

The day thou gavest
You who sleep, rise up, alleluia

A30

As the setting sun
Day is done
Dear Lord and Father of mankind
In your coming and going
I watch the sunrise
I will sing a song
Lord of all hopefulness
Now it is evening
Now the day has drawn to ending
Oh the Word of my Lord
One bread, one body
Round me falls the night
The day thou gavest
You who sleep, rise up, alleluia

Sources

'NH' against a text indicates authorship by Nicholas Hutchinson, FSC

1   David Adam *'The Edge of Glory'*, pg 2, Triangle/SPCK, London, 1985

3   Thomas Merton *'Conjectures of a Guilty Bystander'*, Doubleday Publishers, USA, 1966

6   John Powell, SJ *'Fully Human, Fully Alive'*, pg 92, Tabor Publishing, California, 1976

9   Sir Jacob Astley before the Battle of Edgehill, 1642, in the English Civil War

10   William Barclay *'The William Barclay Prayer Book'*, pg 83, HarperCollins, 1994

11   Teilhard de Chardin, SJ *'Le Milieu Divin'*, HarperCollins, 1992

13   Rabindranath Tagore (1861-1941) *'The Hidden God'* from *'Gintanjali'*, a collection of songs.

14   Misa Campesina of Nicaragua, *'Continent of Hope'*, CAFOD

15   C.I.Pettitt *'A One Hour Service for Good Friday'*, SPCK, London, 1973

18   Roger Schutz, Prior of Taizé, *'A Life We Never Dared Hope For'*, Harper, San Francisco,1984

21   Gerard Hughes, SJ *'In Search of a Way'*, DLT, 1986

22   Gerard Hughes, SJ *'God of Surprises'*, pg 35, DLT, 1985

24   Ian Petit, OSB *'The God who Speaks'*, DLT, 1989

28   Stephen Winward *'How to talk with God'*, Mowbray, Oxford, 1974

30   Stephen Winward *'How to talk with God'*, Mowbray, Oxford, 1974

31   Karl Rahner, SJ *'Encounters with Silence'*, Burns & Oates, London 1961

35   Rita Snowden *'A Woman's Book of Prayers'*, Harper Collins, 1983

36   Jean Vanier, *'Community and Growth'*, pg 67, DLT, 1989

37   Frank Topping *'Pause for Thought with Frank Topping'* pg 229, Lutterworth Press, Guildford, 1981

38   Flor McCarthy, SDB *'Sunday and Holyday Liturgies: Cycle C'* pg 88, Dominican Publications, Dublin, 1985

39   J. Barrie Shepherd *'Diary of Daily Prayer'*, Augsburg Publishing House, Minneapolis, 1981

40   Oswald Chambers *'My Utmost for his Highest'* pg 50, Discovery House Publishers, Michigan, 1926

43   Edward Farrell *'Celtic Meditations'*, Dimension Books, Denville, New Jersey, 1976

44   Terence Collins, FSC based on St Augustine *'Confessions'*, Chapter 1

45   Peter van Breemen, SJ *'As Bread that is Broken'*, Dimension Books, Denville, New Jersey, 1978

47   Peter van Breemen, SJ *'As Bread that is Broken'*, pg 9, Dimension Books, Denville, New Jersey, 1978

51   Louis Evely *'Our Father'*, Herder & Herder, New York, 1970

52   Cardinal Basil Hume *'The Mystery of Love'*, Hodder & Stoughton, London, 1996

54   Margaret Sonnenday *'Images: Women in Transition'*, pg 140, St Mary's Press, Winona, USA: 1977

55   J.B. Phillips *'Letters to Young Churches'* pg 124, HarperCollins, 1955

60   Archbishop Desmond Tutu *'Hope and Suffering'*, pg 137, HarperCollins, 1984

61   Frank Topping *'Wings of the Morning'*, pg 36, Lutterworth Press, Guildford, 1990

62   Jean Vanier *'Be Not Afraid'*, pg 67ff, Gill & Macmillan, Dublin 1975

65   Sheila Cassidy *'Good Friday People'*, pg 72, DLT, 1991

67   Pedro Arrupe, SJ former Jesuit General on his experiences following a stroke (3.9.1983)

70   Cardinal John Henry Newman (1801-90) from *'Meditations on Christian Doctrine'*

71   Teilhard de Chardin, SJ *' Le Milieu Divin'*, HarperCollins, 1992

74   Alfred Monnin *'Life of the Blessed Cure D'Ars'* pg 47, Burns & Oates, London

75   Denis Blackledge, SJ *'Loving Lord: Moments'*, pg 32, Sanctuary Books, Preston, 1991

76   Pope John Paul II during his Pastoral Visit to Great Britain, Bellahouston Park, Glasgow, 1/6/1982

78   Edward Farrell *'Free to be Nothing'*, pg 141, The Liturgical Press, Minnesota, 1989

81   Denis Blackledge, SJ *'Loving Lord: Encounters'*, Sanctuary Books, Preston, 1995

82   Ronald Rolheiser in *'The Catholic Herald'* of 22 October 1993

83   Michel Quoist *'Prayers of Life'*, pg 36, Gill & Macmillan, Dublin, 1963

87   Frank Topping *'Lord of Time'*, Lutterworth Press, Guildford, 1985

88   Bede Griffiths *'The Golden String'*, HarperCollins, London, 1979

89   Frank Topping *'Pause for Thought with Frank Topping'* pg 99, Lutterworth Press, Guildford, 1981

90   Carlo Carretto *'The Desert in the City'*, pg 40, HarperCollins, 1983

91   Frank Topping *'Wings of the Morning'*, pg 33, Lutterworth Press, Guildford, 1990

96   Donal Neary, SJ *'Lighting the Shadows'*, pg 18, Veritas Publications, Dublin, 1995

100   Lucien Deiss *'Come, Lord Jesus'* pg 275, World Library Publications, Chicago, 1981

101   Cardinal Basil Hume, OSB *'To Be a Pilgrim'*, pg 34, St Paul Publications, London, 1984

111   St Gregory of Nyssa *Second Homily on the Song of Songs*

112   The Astronauts' Prayer, read by Frank Borman aboard Apollo 8, 24 December 1968

116   Edward King *'Sermons and Addresses'* pg 37, Longmans, Green & Co., London, 1911

117   Frank Topping *'Pause for Thought with Frank Topping'* pg 131, Lutterworth Press, Guildford, 1981

119   Iona Community *'Iona Community Worship Book'*, pg 40, Wild Goose Publications, Glasgow, 1994

122   William Wordsworth from *'Lines composed a few miles above Tintern Abbey on revisiting the banks of the Wye during a tour. July 13, 1798'*

124   An African Canticle (patterned on Daniel 3:52-90) from *'An African Prayer Book'* edited by Archbishop Desmond Tutu, Bantam, Doubleday Dell, New York, 1995

125   Walter Rauschenbusch *'Selected Writings'*, edited by Winthrop S. Hudson, Paulist Press, New York, 1984

126   Elizabeth Barrett Browning *Aurora Leigh* (1857) Book 7, Line 821

134   F.C.Happold based on *'The Hymn of the Universe'* by Teilhard de Chardin, SJ *'The Journey Inwards'* DLT, 1968

136   Hubert Van Zeller, OSB *'Leave Your Life Alone'* pg 38, Sheed & Ward, London, 1972

138   Edward Farrell *'Gathering the Fragments'*, pg 35, Ave Maria Press, Indiana, 1987

139   *'Catechism of the Catholic Church'* nn. 368, 2562, 2563

141   Frank Colquhoun *'Prayers for Everyone'*, Triangle/SPCK, 1991

147   Richard Harries (Bishop of Oxford) from *'Praise in all our Days'*, a Taizé Prayerbook, Mowbray, Oxford, 1980

148   Mother Teresa *'In the Silence of the Heart'* compiled by Kathryn Spink, pg 42, SPCK, London, 1983

149   John-Paul Gower (aged 14) originally published in *The Catholic Herald*

151   William Wordsworth from *'Lines composed a few miles above Tintern Abbey on revisiting the banks of the Wye during a tour. July 13, 1798'*

154   Frank Topping *'Lord of Time'*, Lutterworth Press, Guildford, 1985

156   William Barclay *'The Gospel of Matthew'*, vol. 2 pg. 359 of *'The Daily Study Bible'*, St Andrew Press, 1969

159   Carlo Carretto *'Love is for Living'* pg. 109, DLT, 1977

161   J.B.Phillips *'Letters to Young Churches'* pg 215, HarperCollins, 1955

163   Pope John Paul II at the site of the detonation of the atomic bomb, Hiroshima, Japan, 1981

168   Terry Waite who was held captive in the Lebanon from 1986-1991

174   Annabel Shilson-Thomas *'Celebrating One World'*, pg 141, CAFOD/Harper Collins, 1998

176   Julia Esquivel, Guatemalan poet and theologian

177   Pope John Paul II in New York, 1979 (cf. Lk 16:19-31)

182   Caryl Micklem *'Contemporary Prayers for Public Worship'*, SCM-Canterbury Press, London, 1967

187   Bishop Timothy Dudley-Smith *'Someone who beckons'*, Hodder & Stoughton, London 1988

189 Pope Paul VI *'Evangelii Nuntiandi'*, para. 80

190 Kevin Lyon *'Psalm-Prayers for Every Mood'*, Columba Press, 1996

193 J.B.Phillips *'Letters to Young Churches'*, pg 127, HarperCollins, 1955

197 Michael Buckley *'The Catholic Prayer Book'*, pg 230, DLT, 1999

199 Pope John Paul II celebrating the Sacrament of the Sick in Southwark Cathedral, London, during his Visit to Britain in May 1982

206 Carlo Carretto *'Letters from the Desert'* pp 139-141, DLT, 1972

207 Bruce Prewer *'Australian Prayers'*, Openbook Direct, Adelaide, Australia 2002

208 Bernard Thorogood *'Everyday Prayers'*, International Bible Reading Association 1978

209 Leslie F Brandt *'Psalms Anew'*, Concordia Publishing House, Missouri, 1986

212 Lucien Deiss *'Come, Lord Jesus'*, pg 289, World Library Publications, Chicago, 1981

213 John Brook *'The School of Prayer'*, a commentary on the Divine Office pg 125, Harper Collins, 1992

216 Donal Neary, SJ *'The Calm Beneath the Storm'*, page 41, Veritas Publications, Dublin, 1993

218 David Adam *'The Open Gate'*, pg 18, Triangle/SPCK, London, 1994

219 Lucien Deiss *'Come, Lord Jesus'*, pg 290, World Library Publications, Chicago 1981

220 Cardinal Jean-Marie Lustiger *'First Steps in Prayer'*, pg 32, HarperCollins, London, 1988

The Publishers are grateful to the following for permission to include copyright material in this publication.
A P Watt Ltd, 20 John Street, London WC1P 2DL on behalf of The Grail.
Augsburg Publishing House/Fortress Press, 426 South 5th Street, Minneapolis. MN 55440
Ave Maria Press, PO.Box 428, Notre Dame, Indiana 46556-0428
Bantam, Doubleday Dell, a division of Random House, Inc., 1540 Broadway, New York, NY 10036
CAFOD, Romero Close, Stockwell Road, London SW9 9TY
Columba Press, 55a Spruce Avenue, Stillorgan Industrial Park, Blackrock, Co. Dublin.
Concordia Publishing House, 3558 South Jefferson Avenue, St. Louis, Missouri 63118
Continuum International Publishing Group Ltd, The Tower Building, 11 York Road, London SE1 7NX
Curtis Brown Literary Agents, Haymarket House, 28/29 Haymarket, London SW1Y 4SP for Frank Topping.
Dimension Books, P.O. Box 811, Denville, New Jersey 07834
Discovery House Publishers, P.O. Box 3566, Grand Rapids, MI 49501
Darton, Longman and Todd Ltd, 1 Spencer Court, 140 Wandsworth High Street, London SW18 4JJ
Dominican Publications, 42 Parnell Square, Dublin 1, Ireland
Doubleday Publishers, a division of Random House, Inc., 1540 Broadway, New York, NY 10036
HarperCollins Publishers Ltd, 77-85 Fulham Palace Road, Hammersmith,London W6 8JB
Hodder & Stoughton, 338 Euston Road, London, NW1 3BH
International Bible Reading Association, 1020 Bristol Road, Selly Oak, Birmingham B29 6LB
Liturgical Press, St. John's Abbey, P.O. Box 7500, Collegeville, MN 56321-7500
Lutterworth Press, PO Box 60, Cambridge, CB1 2NT, England
Openbook Publishers, 205 Halifax Street, Adelaide SA 5000, Australia
Paulist Press, 997 Macarthur Blvd., Mahwah, NJ 07430
Sanctuary Books, 1 Winckley Square, Preston PR1 3JJ
SCM-Canterbury Press Ltd, 9-17 St Alban's Place, London N1 0NX, UK.
Saint Andrew Press, Church Offices, 121 George Street. Edinburgh EH2 4YN
St Mary's Press, 702 Terrace Heights, Winona, MN 55987-1320
St Paul Publications, Middle Green, Slough SL3 6BS
Triangle/SPCK, Holy Trinity Church, Marylebone Road, London NW1 4DU
Veritas Publications, 7/8 Lower Abbey Street, Dublin 1.
Wild Goose Publications, Unit 15, Six Harmony Row, Glasgow G51 3BA
World Library Publications, 3825 N. Willow Road, Schiller Park, IL 60176

Locating Bible Passages

Old Testament

Genesis

Gen 1-2 - Creation.
Gen 3 - Fall.
Gen 4 - Cain & Abel.
Gen 6-9 - Flood.
Gen 11 - Babel.
Gen 12-25 - Abraham.
Gen 22 - Isaac: sacrifice.
Gen 25 - Esau & Jacob.
Gen 28 - Jacob's dream.
Gen 32 - Jacob wrestles with God.
Gen 37-50 - Joseph & brothers.

Exodus

Ex 1 - Enslaved.
Ex 2-40 - Moses.
Ex 2 - Moses kills Egyptian.
Ex 3 - Burning bush.
Ex 3-7 - Moses' mission; 'Yahweh'.
Ex 7-12 - 10 plagues.
Ex 12 - Passover.
Ex 14-15 - Crossing the sea.
Ex 16 - Manna.
Ex 17 - Water from the rock. Moses raises arms in prayer.
Ex 19-40 - Covenant.
Ex 20 - 10 Commandments = *Deut 5*
Ex 23 - Duties to enemies.
Ex 32 - Golden calf.
Ex 33 - God's glory passes by.
Ex 34 - Moses' face shines.
Ex 40 - Led by cloud & fire.

Leviticus

Lev 19^{18} - Love your neighbour as yourself.
Lev 26 - I will be your God.

Numbers

Num 6 $^{23-26}$ - May the Lord let his face shine upon us.

Deuteronomy

Deut 1^{29} - Yahweh has carried you.
Deut 4^{40} - Prosper & live long.
Deut 5 - 10 Commandments = *Ex 20*
Deut 7 - God's blessing.
Deut 8 - Wilderness.
Deut 8-11 - Promised land.
Deut 11 - Write my words on your doorpost
Deut 24 - Justice for the poor.
Deut 26 - Offerings.
Deut 30 - Blessing or curse - choose life and not death

Joshua

Joshua 6 - Jericho.

Judges

Judges 6-8 - Gideon.
Judges 13-16 - Samson.

Ruth

Ruth 1 - Wherever you go...

1 Samuel

1 Sam 1-2 - Hannah's prayer.
1 Sam 3 - Call of Samuel: Speak,Lord,servant listens.
1 Sam 10 - Samuel anoints Saul.
1 Sam 16 - David is anointed.
1 Sam 17 - David & Goliath.
1 Sam 24 - David spares Saul.

2 Samuel

2 Sam 5 - David anointed king.
2 Sam 6 - Ark in Jerusalem.
2 Sam 11 - David & Bathsheba.
2 Sam 12 - Nathan: lamb story.
2 Sam 18-19 - Absalom's death; David mourns.

1 Kings

1 Kings 3 - Solomon asks for wisdom.
        Solomon's judgement.

1 Kings 10 - Queen of Sheba.

1 Kings 17 - Elijah: flour & oil.
        Widow's son raised.

1 Kings 18 - Prophets on Mt Carmel.

1 Kings 19 - Journey to Horeb: "Get up & eat".
        Earthquake, wind & fire: the still small voice
        of God.

1 Kings 21 - Naboth's vineyard.

---

2 Kings

2 Kings 2 - Elijah/chariot/whirlwind.
        Elisha takes up Elijah's mantle.

2 Kings 4 - Widow's oil.
        Elisha raises dead boy.

2 Kings 5 - Naaman's leprosy healed.

---

1 Chronicles

1 Chron 13 - David & Ark.

1 Chron 29 - David's prayer.

---

2 Chronicles

2 Chron 1 - Solomon asks for wisdom.

2 Chron 5 - Ark to Temple.

2 Chron 9 - Queen of Sheba.

---

2 Maccabees

2 Macc 7 - Martyrdom of the 7 brothers.

Job

Job 1,2 - Satan tests Job.

Psalms

Ps 8 - Creation; mankind: when I see work of your hands.

Ps 22(21) - Why have you forsaken me?

Ps 23(22) - The Lord is my shepherd.

Ps 24(23) - Who shall climb Lord's mountain?

Ps 27(26) - Lord is my light & my help.

Ps 31(30) - Into your hands I commend my spirit.

Ps 42/43 - Like the deer that yearns.

Ps 51(50) - Have mercy on me in your kindness

Ps 63(62) - Your love is better than life.

Ps 67(66) - Be gracious and bless us.

Ps 71(70) - Prayer in old age:
        In you, Lord, I take refuge.

Ps 84(83) - How lovely is your dwelling place.

Ps 91(90) - Under the Divine wings:
        He who dwells; I will raise you up.

Ps 95(94) - Today listen to his voice.

Ps 100(99) - Enter courts with songs of praise.

Ps 103(102) - My soul, give thanks to the Lord;
        the Lord is compassion & love.

Ps 104(103) - Splendour of creation:
        Bless the Lord, my soul.

Ps 110(109) - Messiah, King, Priest, Judge.

Ps 112(111) - Good person takes pity and lends.

Ps 113(112) - From rising of sun to its setting. From dust
        he lifts up lowly.

Ps 117(116) - Strong is his love for us.

Ps 118(117) - This is day the Lord has made.

Ps 121(120) - At your right side he stands; he will guard
        going and coming.

Ps 122(121) - Let us go to God's house.

Ps 126(125) - Song of the Return.

Ps 127(126) - If Lord does not build house.

Ps 130(129) - Out of the depths I cry to you.

Ps 131(130) - Like a child.

Ps 134(133) - Night prayer: lift up hands.

Ps 136(135) - For his love endures forever.

Ps 137(136) - By the rivers of Babylon.

Ps 138(137) - Your faithfulness & love; You stretch out
        hand & save me.

Ps 139(138) - God's presence; You search me & know me

Ps 141(140) - Let my prayer rise up like incense before
        you, Lord.

Ps 145(144) - Lord is kind & full of compassion

Ps 146(145) - Lord gives sight to blind & raises up those
        bowed down.

Ps 147(146) - heals the brokenhearted;
        Binds up all their wounds.

Ps 147B - Praise the Lord, Jerusalem.

Ps 148 - He commanded, they were made:
        fire & hail, snow & mist.

Ecclesiastes

Ecc 3 - A season & time for everything.

Proverbs

Prov 29^{18} - Without vision we perish.

Song of Songs

Song 2 - The cry of my beloved.

Wisdom

Wis 3 - The souls of the virtuous are in...

Wis 7 - Respect for wisdom; I prayed & understanding
     was given me.

Wis 11^{23}-12^2 - You love all that exists...

Sirach (Ecclesiasticus)

Sir 2 - If you aspire to serve the Lord, prepare for an
     ordeal.

Sir 6 - Friendship.

Sir 17 - The wonder of mankind.

Sir 24 - Wisdom: I came forth from...

Sir 39 - His memory will not disappear.

Sir 43 - The splendour of nature.

Sir 44 - Let us praise illustrious men.

Isaiah

Is 1 - Though your sins are like scarlet...

Is 2 - Let's go up to Temple of the Lord that he may
     teach us his ways.= *Mic 4*

Is 6 - Holy, holy.

Is 7^{14} - Sign: maiden will be with child.

Is 9 - The people that walked in darkness...
     a child born for us.

Is 11 - A shoot shall spring; wolf with lamb.

Is 25 - Messianic banquet; destroy death & wipe away
     all tears.

Is 35 - Your God is coming; eyes of the blind be opened.

Is 40 - Console my people; prepare the way;
     let every valley; walk & never tire;
     creation - majesty of God;
     put out wings like eagles.

Is 42 - Open eyes of blind.

Is 43 - Do not be afraid: called by name;
     no need to recall the past.

Is 49 - Does a woman forget child?
     name on palms of my hands.

Is 50 - A disciple's tongue;
     I offered my back - struck me.

Is 52 - How lovely on the mountains: one who brings
     good news.

Is 53 - Without beauty or majesty we saw him; he was
     pierced for our faults; like a lamb to slaughter.

Is 55 - Come to the water; word that goes from my mouth
     does not return to me empty.

Is 58 - Liberty to captives, bread to hungry.

Is 61 - Sent me to bring good news to poor,
     liberty to captives.

Is 66 - Rejoice with Jerusalem.

Jeremiah

Jer 1 - Before I formed you in the womb;
     I put my words into your mouth.

Jer 15 - Your word was my delight & the joy of my heart.

Jer 20 - You have seduced me, Lord.

Jer 29^{13} - When you seek me you shall find me.

Jer 31^{31} - I will make a new covenant I will be their God
     & they my people. They will all know me.

Ezekiel

Ezek 11 - I'll gather you -scattered; I'll put new spirit
     in you; heart of stone/flesh.

Ezek 34 - Shepherding…

Ezek 36 - I will pour clean water over you & give you
     new heart/spirit.

Ezek 37 - Dry bones.

Daniel

Dan 3 - young men in furnace.

Dan 5 - Belshazzar's Feast; writing on wall.

Dan 6,14 - Daniel thrown to lions.

Dan 7^{13},10^{16} - "Son of man"

Dan 13 - Susanna; Daniel's judgement.

Hosea

Hos 11 - When Israel was a child I loved him; the more
I called, further they went from me.

Hos 14 - Come back to the Lord.

Joel

Joel 2 - Come back to me; God is tenderness
& compassion.

Joel 3 - I will pour out my spirit;
young men have visions & old men have dreams.

Amos

Am 5 - Hate evil, love good; let justice flow like water,
& integrity like unfailing stream.

Am 7 - Plumb-line.

Am 8 - You who trample on the needy;
tampering with the scales.

Jonah

Jon 1 - Jonah thrown overboard.

Jon 2 - Swallowed by great fish.

Jon 3 - People of Nineveh repent.

Jon 4 - Jonah & castor-oil plant.

Micah

Mic 4 - Let's go up to mountain of Lord that he may
teach us his ways.=*Isaiah 2*
Swords into ploughshares.
Nation not lift up sword...

Mic 6 - My people, what have I done to you?
Act justly, love tenderly, walk humbly with God.

Mic 7^{19} - Tread down our faults; cast them to bottom of sea.

Habbakuk

Hab 3^{17} - Though fig tree doesn't blossom...
yet I will rejoice in the Lord.

Zephaniah

Zeph 3^{17} - Yahweh is in your midst; he will renew you
by his love.

New Testament – Gospels

EVENTS

Early life

Word of Life - Jn 1^{1-18}

Genealogy - Mt 1^{1-17}; Lk 3^{23-38}

Birth & infancy - Mt 1-2; Lk 1-2

John the Baptist - Mt $3^{1-12}, 11^{1-15}$, 14^{1-12}; Mk $1^{1-8}, 6^{14-29}$;
  Lk $1,3^{1-20}, 7^{18-27}$; Jn $1^{19-34}, 3^{22-33}$

Early ministry

Baptism of Jesus -Mt 3^{13-17}; Mk 1^{9-11}; Lk 3^{21-22}

Temptation of Jesus -Mt 3^{13-17}; Mk 1^{12-13}; Lk 4^{1-13}

In Nazareth synagogue - Lk 4^{16-30}

Jesus calls the 12 -Mt $4^{18-22}, 9^9$; Mk $1^{16-20}, 2^{13-14}, 3^{13-19}$;
  Lk $5^{1-11,27-28}, 6^{12-16}$; Jn 1^{35-51}

Other events

Adulterous woman -Jn 8^{1-11}

Cana: wedding -Jn 2^{1-12}

Children: example; greatness - Mt 18^{1-10}, 19^{13-15};
  Mk $9^{33-37,42-50}, 10^{13-16}$; Lk 9^{46-48}, $10^{21-22}, 18^{15-17}$

Cleansing of temple -Mt 21^{12-13}; Mk 11^{15-17}; Lk 19^{45-46};
  Jn 2^{13-25}

Eating with sinners - Mt 9^{10-13}; Mk 2^{13-17}; Lk 5^{29-32}

Martha & Mary -Lk 10^{38-42}

Mission of the 12 -Mt 10^{1-42}; Mk 6^{7-13}; Lk 9^{1-6}

Mission of the 72 -Lk 10^{1-12}

Payment of Temple tax -Mt 17^{24-27}

Peter's profession of faith -Mt 16^{13-20}; Mk 8^{27-30}; Lk 9^{18-21};
  Jn 6^{67-71}

Picking corn on Sabbath - Mt 12^{1-8}; Mk 2^{23-28}; Lk 6^{1-5}

Rejected at Nazareth - Mt 13^{53-58}; Mk 6^{1-6}; Lk 4^{16-30}

Rich young man - Mt 19^{16-26}; Mk 10^{17-27}; Lk 18^{18-30}

Samaritan woman at well - Jn 4^{1-42}

Transfiguration - Mt 17^{1-8}; Mk 9^{2-8}; Lk 9^{28-36}

Widow's Mite - Mk 12^{41-44}; Lk 21^{1-4}

Woman sinner: wipes feet of Jesus - Lk 7^{36-50}

Zacchaeus -Lk 19^{1-10}

Last days

Entry to Jerusalem - Mt 21^{3-11}; Mk 11^{1-22}; Lk 19^{28-38};
  Jn 12^{12-19}

Anointing at Bethany - Mt 26^{6-13}; Mk 14^{3-9}; Jn 12^{1-8}

Last Supper - Mt 26^{17-29}; Mk 14^{12-25}; Lk 22^{7-20};
  (also 1 Cor 11^{23-25})

Gethsemane - Mt 26^{36-56}; Mk 14^{32-52}; Lk 22^{39-53};
  Jn 18^{1-11}

Crucifixion & Resurrection - Mt 27-28; Mk 15-16;
  Lk 23-24; Jn 19-21

Emmaus - Lk 24^{13-35}

Ascension - Lk 24^{50-53} (& ACTS 1^{6-11})

JESUS' TEACHING

(in what follows: *italicised* = in Sermon on Mount,
  being Mt 5-7; Lk 6^{17-49})

Almsgiving - Mt 6^{1-4}

Anxious - Mt 6^{25}

Ask, seek, knock - Mt 7^{7-11}; Lk 11^{9-13}

Barren fig tree - Mt 21^{18-22}; Mk 11^{12-25}

Beatitudes - Mt 5^{1-12}; Lk 6^{20-26}

'Be compassionate/merciful as your Father is' - Lk 6^{36-37}

Birds of the air - Mt 6^{25}

But I say to you - Mt 5^{20-48}

Divorce - Mt $5^{31}, 19^{1-9}$; Mk 10^{1-12}; Lk 16^{18}

Do not let your hearts be troubled - Jn 14^1

Do not worry - Mt 6^{25}

Eye - Mt 6^{22-23}; 7^{3-5}; Lk 6^{41-42}; Lk 11^{34-36});

Faith - Mt 21^{18-22}; (Lk 17^{5-6})

*False prophets & true disciples: by their fruit
  - Mt 7^{15-27}; Lk 6^{43-44};*

Fasting - Mt 6^{16-18}; Mt 9^{14-17}; Mk 2^{18-22}; Lk 5^{33-39}

First/last - Mt 20^{16}

Forgiveness - Mt 18^{21-22}; Lk 17^4

Friends I call you - Jn 15^{16}

Fruit: good/bad - Mt 7[15-20],12[33]; *Lk 6[43-44]*;Jn 15[5]

God loved the world so much - Jn 3[16]

Good shepherd - Jn 10[1-18]

Greatest commandment - Mt 22[34-40]; Mk 12[28-34];
    Lk 10[25-28]

Greatness: being a servant - Mt 20[24-28]; Mk 10[41-45];
    Lk 22[24-27]

Grow greater/smaller - Jn 3[30]

Harvest is rich - Mt 9[36-37]; Lk 10[2]

Home in me - Jn 15[4]

"Hungry,thirsty,naked…" - Mt 25[31-46]

I am - Jn 8[58]

I am bread of life - Jn 6[25-59]

I am gate - Jn 10[7]

I am good shepherd - Jn 10[14]

I am light of world - Jn 8[12],9[5]

I am resurrection - Jn 11[25]

I am vine - Jn 15[1-7]

I am way,truth,life - Jn 14[6]

I call you friends - Jn 15[14]

If anyone is thirsty - Jn 7[37-39]

Increase/decrease - Jn 3[30]

Judging & hypocrisy - Mt 7[1-5]; Lk 6[37-42]

Kingdom of God is among you - Lk 17[21]

Labour, rest, yoke - Mt 11[28-30]

Last Judgement (I was hungry…) - Mt 25[31-46]

Left everything; first/last - Mt 19[27-30]; Mk 10[28-31];
    Lk 18[28-30]

Life in all its fulness - Jn 10[10]

Light - Mt 5[12-16] (see also "Parables - Lamp", and
    "I am light")

Love enemies - Mt 5[38-48]; Lk 6[27-36]

Love one another - jn 13[34],15[12]

Love your neighbour as yourself - Lk 10[27]

Make your home in me - Jn15[4]

Man cannot live on bread alone -Mt 4[4]

My brother/sister/mother - Mt 12[46-50]; Mk 3[31-35]; Lk 8[19-21]

Narrow gate - Mt 7[13-14]; Lk 13[24]

New & old out of storeroom - Mt 13[51-52]

New commandment - Jn 13[34],15[12]

Nicodemus: being born again - Jn 3[1-21]

No greater love a man can have - Jn 15[13]

Not with me is against me - Mt 12[30]

'Our Father' - Mt 6[7-13]; Lk 11[1-4]

Peace I leave with you - Jn 14[27]

Persecution - Mt 10[17-33]

Places of honour at table - Lk 14[7-11]

Plank in eye - Mt 7[3-5]; Lk 6[41-42]

Possessions - Mt 6[24]; Lk 16[13]

Prayer: 2 or 3 gather - Mt 18[19-20]

Prayer in secret - Mt 6[5-6]

Priestly prayer of Jesus - Jn 17

Prophet despised in own country - Mt 13[53-58]; Mk 6[1-6]

Request of James & John - Mt 20[20-28]; Mk 10[35-40]

Resurrection of dead - Mt 22[23-33]; Mk 12[18-27]; Lk 20[27-40]

Riches: eye of needle - Mt 19[23-26]; Mk 10[23-27]

Salt & light of world - Mt 5[13-16]; Mk 9[50]; Lk 14[34-35]

Seek first the kingdom - Mt 6[33]; Lk 12[31]

Sparrows; care - Mt 10[28-31]

Spirit - Lk 4[18], Jn 16[5-15],20[22]

Splinter in eye - Mt7[3-5]; Lk6[41-42]

Take up cross & follow - Mt 10[37-39],16[24-28]; Mk 8[34-38];
    Lk 9[23-26],14[27]

Treat others as - Mt 7[12]

Tribute to Caesar - Mt 22[15-22]; Mk 12[13-17]; Lk 20[20-26]

True treasures - Mt 6[19-21]; Lk 12[33-34]

Trusting in providence, seeing how flowers grow
    - Mt 6[25-34]; Lk 12[22-32]

Truth will set you free - Jn 8[32]

Worried - Mt 6[25]

PARABLES

Coins: silver/gold (talents) - Mt 25^{14-30}; Lk 19^{11-27}

Counting cost: building & fighting -Lk 14^{25-33}

Crafty steward ("write 50") - Lk 16^{1-8}

Darnel(weeds) - Mt 13^{24-30}

Dragnet - Mt 13^{47-50}

Fig tree (unfruitful) - Lk 13^{6-9}

Good Samaritan - Lk 10^{29-37}

Great feast - Mt 22^{1-10}; Lk 14^{15-24}

Growing seed - Mk 4^{26-29}

Labourers in vineyard - Mt 20^{1-16}

Lamp - Mk 4^{21-23}; Lk 8^{16-18},11^{33-36}

Lost coin - Lk 15^{8-10}

Lost sheep - Mt 18^{12-14}; Lk 15^{4-7}

Lost son - Lk 15^{11-32}

Measure - Mk 4^{24-25}

Mustard seed - Mt $13^{31-32,36-43}$; Mk 4^{30-32}; Lk 13^{18-19}

New cloth on old coat - Mt 9^{16}; Mk 2^{21}; Lk 5^{36}

New wine in used wineskins -Mt 9^{17}; Mk 2^{22}; Lk 5^{37-38}

Pearl - Mt 13^{45-46}

Pharisee & tax collector - Lk 18^{9-14}

Prodigal son - Lk 15^{11-32}

Rich fool (barns) - Lk 12^{13-21}

Rich man & Lazarus (having died) - Lk 16^{19-31}

Servant's duty ("done no more than duty") - Lk 17^{7-10}

Sower - Mt 13^{4-23}; Mk 4^{1-20}; Lk 8^{4-15}

Talents [silver/gold coins] -Mt 25^{14-30}; Lk 19^{11-27}

Tenants in vineyard (wicked husbandmen) - Mt 21^{33-46}; Mk 12^{1-12}; Lk 20^{9-19}

Ten bridesmaids - Mt 25^{1-13}

Treasure - Mt 13^{45}

Two housebuilders - Mt 7^{24-27}; Lk 6^{46-49}

Two sons - Mt 21^{28-32}

Unforgiving debtor - Mt 18^{23-35}

Unfruitful fig tree - Lk 13^{6-9}

Watchful servants - Lk 12^{35-48}

Wedding feast (man without wedding clothes) - Mt 22^{1-14}

Widow & Judge - Lk 18^{1-8}

Wise & faithful steward - Mt 24^{45-51}

Yeast - Mt 13^{33}; Lk 13^{20-21}

MIRACLES

People-miracles

Bartimaeus - Mk 10^{46-52}

Blind man at Bethsaida - Mk 8^{22-26}

Blind man/men of Jericho - Mt 20^{29-34}; Mk 10^{46-52} (Bartimaeus); Lk 18^{35-43}

Centurion's servant - Mt 8^{5-13}; Lk 7^{1-10}

Crippled woman on Sabbath - Lk 13^{10-17}

Daughter of Canaanite/Syrophoenician woman healed - Mt 15^{21-28}; Mk 7^{24-30}

Deaf & dumb man - Mk 7^{31-37}

Demoniac - Mk 1^{21-28}; Lk 4^{31-37}

Demoniac, pigs - Mt 8^{28-34}; Mk 5^{1-20}; Lk 8^{26-39}

Dropsical man on Sabbath - Lk 14^{1-6}

Dumb demoniac - Mt 9^{32-34}

Ear of High Priest's slave - Lk 22^{50-51}

Epileptic demoniac - Mt 17^{14-20}; Mk 9^{14-29}; Lk 9^{37-43}

Jairus' daughter raised to life - Mt 9^{18-36}; Mk 5^{21-43}; Lk 8^{40-56}

Lazarus raised - Jn 11

Leper - Mt 8^{1-4}; Mk 1^{40-45}; Lk 5^{12-16}

Man born blind - Jn 9

Official's son in Capernaum ("Go: your son will live") - Jn 4^{43-54}

Paralytic - Mt 9^{1-8}; Mk 2^{1-12}; Lk 5^{17-26}

Sick touch fringe of cloak - Mt 14^{34-36}

Sick man at Sheep Pool in Jerusalem - Jn 5^{1-18}

Simon Peter's mother-in-law - Mt 8^{14-15}; Mk 1^{29-31}; Lk 4^{38-39}

Ten lepers - Lk 17^{11-19}

Two blind men - Mt 9^{27-31}

Widow of Nain's son raised - Lk 7^{11-17}

Withered hand - Mt 12^{9-14}; Mk 3^{1-6}; Lk 6^{6-11}

Woman with haemorrhage - Mt 9^{18-26}; Mk 5^{21-43}; Lk 8^{40-56}

Nature-miracles

Calming of storm - Mt 8^{23-27}; Mk 4^{35-41}; Lk 8^{22-25}

Cana: water into wine - Jn 2^{1-11}

Catches of fish - Lk 5^{1-11}; and Jn 21^{1-11}

Feeds 4000 - Mt 15^{32-39}; Mk 8^{1-10}

Feeds 5000 - Mt 14^{13-21}; Mk 6^{30-44}; Lk 9^{10-17}; Jn 6^{1-15}

Walks on water - Mt 14^{22-33}; Mk 6^{45-52}; Jn 6^{16-21}

New Testament – Acts, Letters

ACTS

Acts 1$^{6-11}$ - Ascension (& Lk 24$^{50-53}$)

Acts 2 - Pentecost.

Acts 2$^{42-47}$ - Early Christian community: faithful to teaching, brotherhood, breaking of bread.

Acts 3 - Cure of cripple:"Neither silver/gold".

Acts 4$^{32-35}$ - Early Christian community

Acts 5$^{12-16}$ - Signs & wonders; shadow of Peter.

Acts 5$^{22-33}$ - Obedience to God/men

Acts 5$^{34-42}$ - Gamaliel: if of human origin/if from God.

Acts 6$^{1-7}$-7 -helpers.

Acts 6^{8}-8^3 - Stephen's death; "Saul approved".

Acts 8$^{9-25}$ - Simon the magician: simony.

Acts 9$^{1-31}$ - Conversion of Saul (Paul): (Paul's own account: 22$^{6-21}$, 26$^{12-18}$; Gal 1^{11}-2^{10})

Acts 9$^{36-43}$ - Tabitha raised to life in Jaffa.

Acts 10^1-11^{18}- Centurion Cornelius & Peter's Dream: God has no favourites (& 11$^{1-18}$; Gal 2^6).

Acts 11^{26} - At Antioch: first called Christians.

Acts 12$^{1-19}$ -Peter's arrest & deliverance: angel.

Acts 13$^{4-12}$ -Fraudulent Elymas is blinded.

Acts 14$^{8-18}$ -Cripple healed: Paul & Barnabas about to be worshipped.

Acts 16$^{16-40}$- Miraculous deliverance of Paul & Silas: earthquake; gaoler converted.

Acts 17^{28} - In him we live & move & have our being.

Acts 20$^{7-12}$ -Eutychus falls from window; raised to life.

Acts 20^{35} - "More happiness in giving than receiving."

LETTERS

Romans

Rom 5$^{1-11}$ - Faith guarantees salvation; sufferings bring patience, perseverance, hope; Christ died for us while we were still sinners.

Rom 6$^{5-11}$ - Having died with Christ we shall return to life with him. Dead to sin; alive to God.

Rom 7$^{14-25}$ - I fail to carry out what I want to do.

Rom 8$^{1-11}$ - No condemnation for those in Jesus Christ.

Rom 8$^{14-17}$ - Moved by Spirit: 'Abba, Father'. Heirs of God, sharing Christ's sufferings.

Rom 8$^{18-27}$ - What we suffer in this life. Freeing of all creation. Spirit helps us in our weakness.

Rom 8$^{28-30}$ - God turns everything to their good.

Rom 8$^{31-39}$ - With God on our side, could anyone condemn?
Nothing can come between us & Christ's love.
Trials through which we triumph.
Neither death nor life....

Rom 10$^{9-13}$ - If you confess that Jesus is Lord...

Rom 11$^{33-36}$ - How rich are depths of God.

Rom 12$^{3-13}$ - If your gift is...then use it.
Don't let love be a pretence.
Don't give up if trials come.
Make hospitality special care.

Rom 12$^{14-21}$ - Bless those who persecute you.
Resist evil & conquer with good.

Rom 13$^{1-7}$ - Obey civil authority.

Rom 13$^{8-10}$ - Debt of mutual love.

Rom 14$^{7-12}$ - Life & death of each of us has its influence on others.
If we live, we live for the Lord.

---

1 Corinthians

1 Cor 1$^{17-31}$ - Cross is illogical to....

1 Cor 3$^{5-15}$ - Fellow-workers with God; foundation is Jesus.

1 Cor 3$^{16-17}$ - You are God's temple.

1 Cor 4^{10} - Fools for Christ; scum of earth.

1 Cor 9^{22} - All things to all men.

1 Cor 11$^{20-27}$ - The Lord's Supper.

1 Cor 12$^{1-31}$ - Variety of gifts; same Spirit; analogy of the body.

1 Cor 12^{31}-14^1 - LOVE is…

1 Cor 15 - Resurrection; perishable nature;
Death: victory? Sting? By God's grace I am what I am.

2 Corinthians

2 Cor 1[1-11] - God comforts us that we may comfort others.

2 Cor 3 - You are letter from Christ/Spirit.

2 Cor 3[18] - With unveiled faces we reflect God's brightness, & are turned into image we reflect.

2 Cor 4 - Not ourselves we preach.
We are earthenware jars; power comes from God.

2 Cor 5[16-21] - God reconciled us to himself.
In Christ we are a new creation.
Ambassadors for Christ.

2 Cor 6[3-10] - Fortitude in times of suffering; said to be dying & here are alive; with nothing, though everything.

2 Cor 7[10] - To suffer in God's way.

2 Cor 9[6-15] - Thin sowing/reaping.

2 Cor 11[21]-12[12] - God's grace enough for you; his power best in weakness.
Paul's own sufferings. When weak then I am strong.

Galatians

Gal 2[11-14] - Paul disagrees with Peter.

Gal 2[19-20] - I've been crucified with Christ & live now with Christ's life.

Gal 4[1-7] - God sent his Son, born of woman.
Spirit cries 'Abba, Father': you are a son & heir.

Gal 5 - Christian freedom in Spirit.
Love, joy, peace, patience....

Ephesians

Eph 1 - Blessed be God and Father....

Eph 2[1-10] - God loved us with so much love; how infinitely rich in grace.
Saved by grace, through faith.
We are God's work of art.

Eph 3[14-21] - Out of his infinite glory, may he give you...power to grow strong; planted in love; breadth, length...

Eph 4[1-8] - Worthy of your vocation.
One Lord/faith/baptism...
Varied gifts for Body of Christ: to be apostles, prophets, teachers...

Eph 4[17-32] - Give up old way of life; spiritual revolution; put on new self.

Eph 6[10-20] - Put on God's armour.

Philippians

Phil 2[1-11] - Jesus didn't cling to his equality, but emptied himself.

Phil 2[12-18] - God puts will & action into you.
Shine in world like bright stars: you are offering it the word of life.

Phil 3[6-14] - I look on everything as rubbish if I can know Christ & power of resurrection.
I run the race...

Phil 4[4-9] - I want you to be happy in Lord.
Fill your minds with everything that's true, noble, good, pure.

Colossians

Col 1[13-20] - Taken us out of power of darkness & created a place for us in Kingdom.
He is image of invisible God...

Col 1[24-29] - Servant of the Church.
Mystery is Christ among you.
I struggle wearily on: his power drives me irresistibly.

Col 3[5-17] - You have put on a new self.
God's chosen race -he loves you.
Bear with one another.
Let Christ's message find home in you.

Col 3[24] - It is Christ that you are serving.

1 Thessalonians

1 Thess 4[13]-5[11] - Those who have died.
Children of light;
Lord's Day.

1 Thess 5[12-22] - Be happy. Pray constantly.
Give thanks.

2 Thessalonians

2 Thess 3$^{6-15}$ - Some living in idleness; give no food to those who refuse to work.

---

1 Timothy

1 Tim 4$^{12-16}$ - Don't let people disregard you because you are young; use your spiritual gifts.

1 Tim 6^{10} - Love of money is root of all evil.

1 Tim 6$^{11-14}$ - Your aims & fight good fight.

---

2 Timothy

2 Tim 1$^{6-9}$ - Fan into a flame God's gifts.

2 Tim 2$^{1-13}$ - If we have died with him... He is faithful.

2 Tim 3$^{1-5}$ - Outward appearance of religion; inner power.

2 Tim 4$^{1-5}$ - Refute falsehood, shun novelties.

2 Tim 4$^{6-8}$ - I have fought the good fight

Philemon

Philem 1$^{1-25}$ - Runaway slave.

Hebrews

Heb 1$^{1-4}$ - At various times in past, God spoke... but now through his Son, who is radiant light of God's glory.

Heb 4^{12} - Word of God alive and active.

Heb 5$^{1-10}$ - He offered up prayer & entreaty. Although Son, obeyed through suffering.

Heb 11$^{1-40}$ - FAITH of our ancestors...

Heb 12$^{1-4}$ - Many witnesses in cloud around us.

Heb 13^{1} - Welcome strangers (are angels?)

James

Jas 1$^{1-7}$ - Be happy when trials come.

Jas 1$^{22-27}$ - Hearers & do-ers: putting word into practice.

Jas 2$^{1-13}$ - Respect for the poor.

Jas 2$^{12-26}$ - Faith & good works.

Jas 5$^{13-18}$ - Anointing of the sick.

1 Peter

1 Pet 1$^{3-9}$ - Faith tested like gold. You didn't see him, yet love him.

1 Pet 2$^{9-10}$ - Chosen race, royal priesthood, consecrated nation, people apart.

1 Pet 2^{17} - Respect God; honour Emperor.

1 Pet 2$^{18-24}$ - Christ suffered for you: example. By his wounds you are healed.

1 Pet 3^{9} - Pay back with a blessing.

1 Pet 4$^{7-11}$ - Each has received special grace.

1 Pet 4$^{12-19}$ - Suffering as Christians.

1 Pet 5$^{5-11}$ - Unload all your worries; devil prowling around.

---

2 Peter

2 Pet 3$^{8-10}$ - With Lord 1 day = 1000 years

---

1 John

1 Jn 1$^{1-3}$ - We have seen & touched the Word who is life.

1 Jn 1$^{5-7}$ - God is light.

1 Jn 1$^{8-10}$ - If we say we've no sin in us...

1 Jn 3^{1} - Think of the love Father has lavished on us.

1 Jn 4$^{7-21}$ - God is love: God loved us first.

1 Jn 4^{18} - Perfect love drives out fear.

REVELATION

Rev 1$^{4-8}$ - Washed away our sins with his blood: we're kings & priests. Alpha & Omega (+ 21^{6},22^{13})

Rev 3$^{14-22}$ - I stand at door & knock.

Rev 5$^{9-13}$ - Worthy to take scroll. Power, riches, wisdom, strength.

Rev 7$^{9-17}$ - Huge number: persecuted in washed robes.

Rev 12$^{1-17}$ - Sign: pregnant woman; dragon.

Rev 14$^{13-20}$ - On dying. Angel; sickle.

Rev 15$^{3-4}$ - Great & wonderful your works.

Rev 19$^{5-10}$ - Wedding-feast of the Lamb.

Rev 21$^{1-8}$ - New heaven & new earth. Here God lives among men. He will wipe away all tears.

Rev 22^{2} - Leaves of tree for healing of nations.

Rev 22^{17} - Spirit & Bride say: 'Come'. All who are thirsty: 'Come'.

Locating some prayers and readings by phrases

Index (the numbers refer to items, not pages)